No-Time
PARTY
CAKES

No-Time

PARTY
CAKES

CAROL DEACON

Simple to make – Fun to decorate

NEW
HOLLAND

Contents

Introduction

The trouble with birthdays, anniversaries and Christmas is that they keep on coming. Just when you think you've made the ultimate cake for a celebration, another occasion appears on the horizon and you're back to square one, thinking 'What on earth shall I make for them this year?'

Hopefully, this book will inspire you with enough suggestions and ideas to keep all your family and friends in cakes for a long time to come, with the minimum of fuss or purchase of expensive cake decorating equipment on your part.

Feel free to alter and adapt the designs or invent shortcuts wherever you wish. For instance, if you are in a hurry and don't wish to cover a cake board, then simply leave it plain. If you don't have time to make lots of characters, then just make one. If you have another technique you are more familiar with, perhaps for making roses, use that instead of the one I suggest. There is no ultimate 'right' way of doing things – just use the method you feel happiest with and make your own unique creation.

Above all, don't be scared of having a go. At the end of the day, it's just cake and icing and if it really starts to give you grief, just eat it!

Fairy-tale castle

Although this cake is a lot easier to make than it looks, you do have to allow drying time for the turrets (preferably overnight). Once you have mastered gelatin icing, a whole new world of standing models opens up.

■ INGREDIENTS

- 1 quantity gelatin icing (see page 99)
- Cornflour
- 18 cm (7 in) round sponge cake
- 1 quantity buttercream (see page 98)
- Icing sugar
- 700 g (1 lb 8 oz) white sugarpaste
- 10 g (¼ oz) brown sugarpaste
- 40 g (1¾ oz) black sugarpaste
- 1 quantity white royal icing (see page 99)
- 2 edible silver balls
- 25 mini marshmallows
- 6 ice cream cones
- Two 30 g (1 oz) bags white chocolate buttons or similar
- Green food colour (ideally gooseberry green but not essential)
- 1 sheet rice paper
- 70 g (2½ oz) green-coloured coconut (see page 98)

■ UTENSILS

- 6 cardboard tubes (5 kitchen roll inner tubes and one from a roll of tin foil are ideal. Please don't use toilet rolls!)
- Cling film
- Rolling pin
- Small sharp knife
- Water and paintbrush
- Carving knife
- 30 cm (12 in) square cake board
- Ruler
- 4 piping bags (minimum)
- Number 2 piping nozzle
- Scissors
- Small sieve

1 Begin by making the turrets. Cover all the cardboard tubes with cling film and dust lightly with cornflour. Make up the gelatin icing as shown on page 99 and place in a polythene bag. Dust the worksurface with cornflour. Pull off a lump of icing about 130 g (4¼ oz) and roll out no thicker than 3 mm (⅛ in). Cut out a rectangle about 14 cm x 16 cm (5½ in x 6 ½ in). Place the excess icing back in the bag.

Wrap the icing round one of the thicker tubes and secure the join with a little water *(fig 1)*. Place to dry (seam side down) on a spare cake board or similar. Make another four the same size and one shorter one using the thinner tube. The smaller turret should be about 8 cm (3 in) in length.

After about 4-6 hours of drying, the turrets should feel hard on the outside. Carefully slide them off their supports and stand them upright so the centres can dry out. Leave overnight.

2 Level the top of the cake and place it upside down in the middle of the board. Slice and fill the centre with buttercream. Spread a thin layer of buttercream over the top and sides.

3 Dust the worksurface with icing sugar. Roll out and cover the cake with 500 g (1 lb 2 oz) of white sugarpaste. Smooth the top and sides and trim any excess from the base. Press a clean ruler horizontally three or four times around the sides of the cake *(fig 2)*. Then use the back of a knife to make the vertical marks for the bricks.

4 When dry, place a long and short turret together on top of the cake. Ensure the seams are at the back and secure them using royal icing. To provide extra support, roll 30 g (1 oz) of white sugarpaste into a sausage about 28 cm (11 in) long. Paint a light line of water around the base of the two turrets and, starting from the back, press the sausage in place *(fig 3)*.

5 To make two doors, thinly roll out the brown sugarpaste and cut out two rounded, arched shapes. Press a few vertical lines into each one with the back of a knife. Stick the largest door on the front of the cake and the other on the front of the tallest turret. Make two steps in front of each door by sticking two small ovals of

4

6

white sugarpaste on top of each other (*fig 4*). Stick an edible silver ball on the front of each door with a little royal icing.

6   Stick about 25 mini marshmallows around the perimeter of the cake with royal icing. (If you cannot find mini marshmallows in the supermarket, cut up a sausage of sugarpaste instead.)

7   Take two of the ice cream cones. Break little pieces off the base if necessary to help them stand upright. Pipe a thin line of royal icing around the top edges of both turrets and then stick the cones carefully in place on top.

You may find that you have to break a little 'bite' shape out of one side of the cone that goes on top of the shorter turret

so that it can sit snugly against the taller turret (*fig 5*).

8   Neaten the base of each cone with a line of white chocolate buttons stuck on with dabs of royal icing.

9   Place the four remaining gelatin cylinders around the cake. Secure with royal icing and top each one with a cone and line of buttons as before.

10 To make the windows on the turrets, thinly roll out the black sugarpaste and cut out eight narrow rectangles. Keep the leftover icing. Cut one end of each rectangle into a point. Stick one on each turret and two either side of the front door.

Place a little white royal icing in a piping bag fitted with the number 2 icing nozzle. Pipe a neat line from the top to the bottom of a window (*fig 6*). Then pipe a line across the window. Repeat on all the rest. (Leave the windows bare if you find this too tricky.)

5

TIP
If the cake is for someone's birthday, make some extra rocks. Stick them at the front of the board to use as candle holders.

11 To make the rocks, partially knead together 100 g (4 oz) of white sugarpaste and 10 g (¼ oz) of black. Pull off irregular lumps and stick these on the board around the cake using a little water.

12 Colour 45 ml (3 tbsp) of royal icing green. Place half into a piping bag fitted with the number 2 piping nozzle and pipe wiggly lines for the ivy stems all over the cake. Place the rest of the icing in a second bag and snip 3 mm (⅛ in) off the end of the bag. Press the end of the bag against a stem, squeeze lightly then pull the bag away. This should make a simple leaf shape. Continue all over the cake. Practise this first on a sheet of greaseproof paper if you are not very confident.

13 To make the flags, cut six small triangles out of the sheet of rice paper. Pipe a dot of royal icing on the top of one of the cones. Stick a small ball of sugarpaste on top and pipe another dot on top of that. Press one of the triangles into the sugarpaste (*fig 7*). Repeat on the other five cones.

14 Moisten the exposed cake board with a little water and sprinkle the coloured coconut around the base of the cake. To add snow, place a spoonful of icing sugar in a small sieve and sprinkle over the cake.

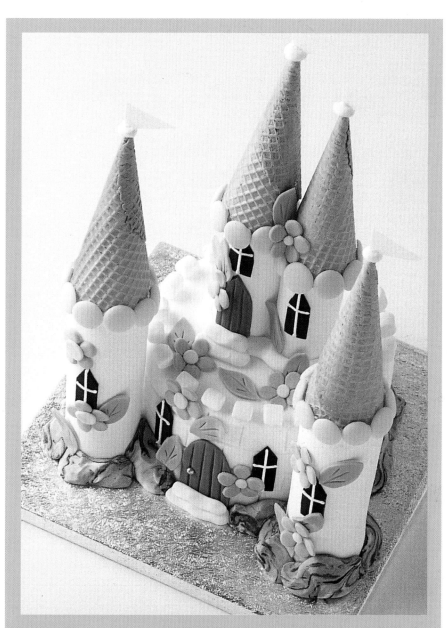

Decorating variation

In this simplified version there are only four turrets instead of six, which saves you time. Also, instead of piping leaves, I have used cut-out flowers and leaves which look just as good. You could also place little figures in front of the top turrets. Use the couple featured on the Bride and Groom cake on page 57 for instance and it turns into a stunning wedding cake with a difference.

Hot dog

How do you like yours? With or without mustard ... er... sorry, icing! Here's one mega bite-sized dog complete with all the trimmings that should satisfy a whole army of hungry party goers.

■ INGREDIENTS

- Icing sugar for rolling out
- 180 g (6¼ oz) dark blue sugarpaste
- Oblong sponge cake baked in loaf tin (see page 94)
- 1 quantity buttercream (see page 98)
- 800 g (1 lb 12 oz) light golden brown sugarpaste
- Assorted food colour pastes for painting sausage (see step 5)
- 100 g (3½ oz) white sugarpaste
- 15 ml (1 tbsp) yellow-coloured buttercream or royal icing
- 15 ml (1 tbsp) red-coloured buttercream or royal icing

■ UTENSILS

- Water and paint brush
- Rolling pin
- Small sharp knife
- Carving knife
- Palette or saucer
- 2 piping bags (see page 102)
- Scissors

1 Cover the cakeboard with blue sugarpaste as described on page 100. Trim and neaten the edges. Place the covered board to one side. Stand the cake the right way up and cut a groove lengthways out of the centre *(fig 1)*.

2 Round the corners slightly and cut away any rough, uneven bits of cake from the tops and sides. Slice and spread a layer of buttercream in the centre of the cake if you wish. Carefully reassemble the cake and spread buttercream over the top and sides and into the groove.

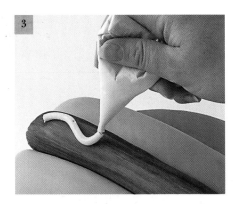

3 Still keeping the cake away from the covered board, knead 600 g (1 lb 5 oz) of the brown sugarpaste until pliable. Roll it out on a surface well dusted with icing sugar, then lift and place over the cake, allowing the sugarpaste to fall into the dip in the middle as much as possible. Starting from the middle of the cake to expel as much air as possible, smooth and ease the icing into position *(fig 2)*. Neaten the sides and trim away any excess from the base. Keep the left-over icing to add to the sausage later.

4 Carefully lift and place the cake on the covered board. Choose the side that looks best and press about six diagonal lines into that side using the back of a knife.

5 Roll the left-over brown sugarpaste into a thick sausage shape, then lay this across the dip. Press a few lines into the ends of the sausage with the back of a knife and to give it a luscious just-cooked look, paint the sausage using food colour. I found a mixture of watered-down dark brown, chestnut and autumn leaf food colour pastes worked well, but you could achieve the same effect by mixing brown with a touch of yellow, red or orange.

6 For the napkin, thinly roll out the white sugarpaste and cut two strips 28 cm x 8 cm (11 in x 3 in). Moisten the board and the base of the cake. Take one strip and lay it down one side of hot dog, allowing it to fall into folds. Repeat on the other side.

7 Make up two piping bags. Place the yellow-coloured royal icing or buttercream in one bag and the red in the other. Pipe a long squiggly line of yellow 'mustard' along the top of the sausage *(fig 3)*. Repeat using the red 'ketchup'.

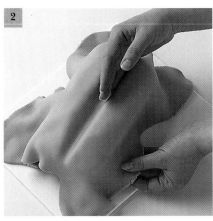

TIP
You may be able to find packs containing small tubes of red and yellow 'writing icing' in your local supermarket which could be used for the mustard and ketchup. Snip a little bit extra off the end of the tube to make the nozzle wider.

Handyman

Although this was designed with do-it-yourself fanatics in mind, this would make a good cake for someone who's just moved house and has all the joys of decorating ahead! Personalize the figure to resemble the recipient if you can.

■ INGREDIENTS

- 15 cm (6 in) square sponge cake
- 1 quantity buttercream (see page 98)
- Icing sugar for rolling out
- 500 g (1 lb 2 oz) white sugarpaste
- 90 g (3 oz) blue sugarpaste
- 20 g (¾ oz) flesh-coloured sugarpaste
- Black food colour paste
- 30 g (1 oz) black sugarpaste
- 10 g (¼ oz) grey sugarpaste
- 110 g (3¾ oz) dark brown sugarpaste

■ UTENSILS

- Carving knife
- 20 cm (8 in) square cake board
- Palette knife
- Small sharp knife
- Water and fine and medium paintbrushes
- Piping nozzle

1 Level the top of the cake, turn it upside down and place in the centre of the board. Slice the cake in half and fill the centre with buttercream. Reassemble the cake and spread a thin covering of buttercream around the top and sides.

2 Knead and roll out 400 g (14 oz) of white sugarpaste on a worksurface dusted with icing sugar. Carefully lay the icing over the cake. Smooth the icing into place and trim and neaten the base.

3 To construct the handyman himself, begin with the body. Roll 40 g (1¼ oz) of white sugarpaste into a cone *(fig 1)*. Paint a little water in the middle of the cake and place his body in position. Next make his legs by rolling 40 g (1¼ oz) of blue sugarpaste into a sausage about 17 cm (7 in) long. Cut the sausage in half and bend the left leg slightly at the knee. Stick the legs in front of the body. For the arms, roll 20 g (¾ oz) of white sugarpaste into a thin sausage and cut it in half. Stick these either side of the handyman's body.

4 To make his head, use 10 g (¼ oz) of flesh-coloured sugarpaste and roll this into a ball. Slice a little icing off the top of his head to make a flat surface on which to attach the cap. Stick the head on top of the body. Flatten two tiny balls of white sugarpaste and stick these onto his face for his eyes. Add a tiny ball of flesh-coloured sugarpaste for his nose. Paint the pupils on the eyes and a smile on his face using black food colour and a fine paintbrush.

5 Partially mix a tiny amount of black sugarpaste with a little white for his hair. Scrunch and tear the icing into little bits and stick them to the sides of his head. Make a little cap by rolling 10 g (¼ oz) of white sugarpaste into a thick disc shape. Pinch and pull the icing on one side to form a peak. Stick this on his head. Finish off the head by sticking two tiny balls of flesh-coloured sugarpaste either side of the head for his ears. Add a little detail by making a small dent in each one with the end of a paintbrush.

6 Roll two 10 g (¼ oz) lumps of black sugarpaste into two oval shapes for his feet and stick one on the end of each leg.

7 To make the paint pot, roll 10 g (¼ oz) of grey sugarpaste into a stumpy cylindrical shape. Press an icing nozzle or something similar into the side to leave a semi-circular impression for the handle. Place the pot between his legs.

For the paintbrush, make two tiny oblongs of brown sugarpaste and one of black. Stick them together like an upside-down 'T' shape and press lines into the black one with a knife to make bristles. Place the brush just in front of the handyman's left arm. Use two small flattened balls of flesh-coloured sugarpaste for his hands and stick these as though he is holding the paint pot and brush.

8 To make the planks of wood, roll 100 g (3½ oz) of dark brown sugarpaste and 20 g (¾ oz) of white together into a sausage.

Fold the sausage in half and roll again. Keep rolling and folding to achieve a woodgrain effect. Roll out the icing and cut out strips of varying lengths *(fig 2)*. Stick a few on and around the cake.

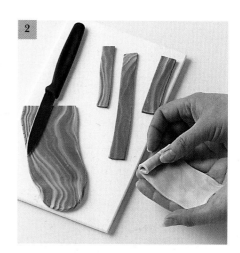

9 To make the rolls of wallpaper, partially knead 50 g (2 oz) of blue sugarpaste and 20 g (¾ oz) of white together to achieve a marbled effect. Carefully roll the sugarpaste out and cut out two strips. Roll one strip up completely and the other about halfway. Stick them onto the cake.

Finally, dab splodges of black food colour around the cake and on the character himself.

Wild animals

My nephew Jack helped with the colours of this cake. 'Potamusses are grey', he informed me gravely, but to balance the cake, they had to be brown. However Jack pointed out, 'That's why they're in the water – because they're all covered in mud!'

INGREDIENTS

- 20 cm (8 in) round sponge cake
- 1 quantity buttercream (see page 98)
- Icing sugar for rolling out
- 700 g (1 lb 8½ oz) white sugarpaste
- 150 g (5¼ oz) grey sugarpaste
- Black food colour
- 100 g (3½ oz) brown sugarpaste
- 20 g (½ oz) green sugarpaste
- Dark brown, gooseberry green and ice blue (or similar) food colour pastes
- 45 ml (3 tbsp) white royal icing (optional)
- 30 g (1 oz) black sugarpaste

UTENSILS

- Carving knife
- 25 cm (10 in) round cake board
- Rolling pin
- Small sharp knife
- Water and paintbrush
- Drinking straw
- Icing nozzle
- Large brush or pastry brush
- Piping bag
- Scissors

1 Shape the cake by cutting bits off the top to leave an irregular surface. Try to leave a flattish area towards the front of the cake for the 'lake'. Spread some of the cut-away pieces of cake with buttercream and build up a small hill behind the lake *(fig 1)*.

2 Place the cake on the cake board and slice and fill the centre with buttercream. Reassemble the cake and spread a covering of buttercream over the sides and top. Keep any leftover buttercream if you are going to use this for the lake and greenery instead of royal icing. Sprinkle the worksurface with icing sugar and knead 500 g (1 lb 2 oz) of white sugarpaste until pliable. Roll out the sugarpaste, then lift and place it over the cake. Carefully smooth the icing into position.

3 To make life easier, construct the elephants, hippos and crocodile away from the cake and place in position later. For the elephants, first roll out 10 g (¼ oz) of grey sugarpaste to a thickness of about 1 cm (⅜ in) and cut out two discs. Make four small vertical cuts at quarterly intervals around the edge of each disc for the legs *(fig 2)*. Roll two 40 g (1 ½ oz) lumps of grey sugarpaste into two balls for

the bodies. Press gently on the front of each ball to make a slope on which to rest the head. Stick one ball onto each set of legs, making sure that both the slope and one of the small cuts are facing forward.

4 To make the heads, roll two 20 g (¾ oz) lumps of grey sugarpaste into chunky tennis racquet shapes. Stick one onto each body. Add nostrils by pushing the end of a paintbrush twice into the end of each trunk. Also press a couple of lines across each trunk with the back of a knife. To make the ears, roll about 5 g (⅛ oz) of grey sugarpaste into a ball. Flatten the ball and cut in half. Moisten the sides of the elephant's head and stick the ears in position. Repeat for the other elephant.

   To make a tail, roll a tiny ball of grey sugarpaste into a thin string and stick it onto the rear of the elephant. Finally, stick two tiny discs of white sugarpaste on each face for eyes. Paint in the pupils and eyebrows with black food colour.

5 To make the biggest hippo, roll 30 g (1 oz) of brown sugarpaste into a semi-circular shape for his body *(fig 3)*. Add a head by

rolling 10 g (¼ oz) of brown sugarpaste into an oval. Squeeze the centre of the oval slightly and stick onto the body. Stick two tiny brown balls onto the sides of the head for ears and add detail to each one by making a small hollow with the end of a paintbrush. Paint two tiny dots of black food colour for the eyes. Make a smaller version for the baby.

   To make the submerged hippo, simply roll 10 g (¼ oz) brown sugarpaste into an oval and flatten the base so it can stand upright. Add ears and eyes.

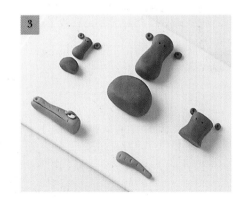

6 For the crocodile, roll 10 g (¼ oz) of green sugarpaste into a sausage about 6 cm (2½ in) long. Try to make the ends slightly thicker than the middle (*fig 3*). Press a line around the base of the sausage to make a mouth and add scales by pressing a drinking straw held at an angle into the icing. Also poke two dents for nostrils using the end of a paintbrush.

7 To make his eye, stick a tiny flattened oval of white sugarpaste onto the side of the head and finish off with an eyebrow made from a tiny strip of green sugarpaste bent into an 'S' shape and stuck over the eye. Add a small dot of black food colour for the pupil.

   To make the tail, roll the remaining green sugarpaste into a long, tapering triangular shape and press a few scales into the sides, as on the head.

8 Using a fairly large paint- or pastry brush, paint the back of the cake using watered-down brown and green food colour (*fig 4*). (I used dark brown and gooseberry green food colour pastes for this but anything similar will do.) Place the elephants into position on the 'grass' while it is still wet.

9 Partially mix a little blue food colour into about 30 ml (2 tbsp) of white royal icing or buttercream if you prefer a softer finish. Swirl this over the front section of the top of the cake and place the hippos and

crocodile sections into position.

10 To make a monkey, roll 10 g (¼ oz) of brown sugarpaste into a cone (*fig 5*). Stick this against the side of the cake and add a brown sugarpaste ball on top for his head.

   For his features, make two tiny balls and an oval shape out of white sugarpaste. Flatten all three shapes and stick the two white discs on top of the head for his eyes and the oval just below for his muzzle. Press the edge of an icing nozzle or

something similar into the muzzle to make a smiling impression and paint three dots for the eyes and the nose with black food colour. Stick two tiny balls of brown sugarpaste either side of the head for his ears and make a small hollow into each one with the end of a paintbrush.

   For the arms, make two small sausages of brown sugarpaste and stick these in whatever position you wish. Make another monkey for the other side of the cake.

11 To make the rocks, take 170 g (6 oz) of white sugarpaste and 30 g (1 oz) of black. Partially knead the two lumps together (*fig 6*). Pull off small irregular lumps and stick these around the base of the cake and a few on top.

12 Colour about 15 ml (1 tbsp) of royal icing or buttercream green. Place the coloured icing into a piping bag and secure the end. Snip about 3 mm (⅛ in) off the pointed end of the bag and pipe a few strands of foliage around the rocks on the sides and top of the cake (*fig 7*).

TIP

If you're really short of time but still want to make a cake in this style, raid your local sweet shop or the confectionery counter at a large supermarket for jelly animal sweets. Either substitute these for the modelled animals or add to the animals in the scene.

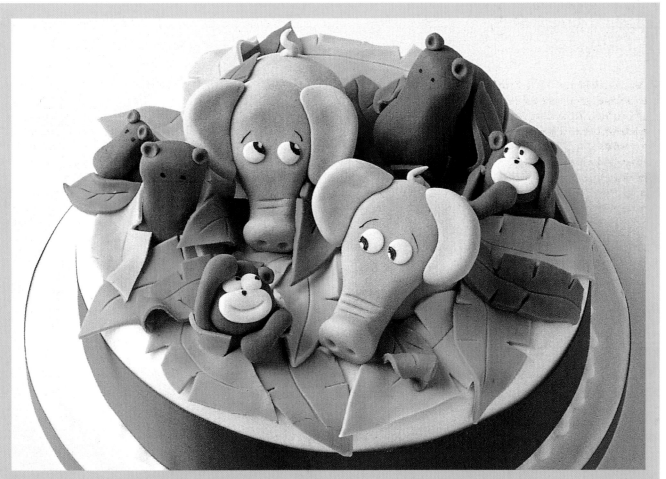

D e c o r a t i n g   v a r i a t i o n

In this simplified version, the basic cake was covered in the same way as the Christening cake on page 50. The animals were modelled as described above, then surrounded by simple jungle-type leaves made from several shades of green sugarpaste. Details for making these are given in the Sunbather cake on page 82.

Birthday fairy

Here's someone who should brighten up any girl's birthday. If you want to cheat, your local cake decorating shop should stock plastic figures made for inserting into cakes, although they may not have as much personality as this one!

■ INGREDIENTS

- 1 pudding bowl cake (see page 94)
- ½ quantity buttercream (see page 98)
- Icing sugar for rolling out
- 400 g (14 oz) white sugarpaste
- 3 candy sticks (or sweet cigarettes as they used to be called)
- 20 g (¾ oz) flesh-coloured sugarpaste
- Black food colour paste
- 20 g (¾ oz) yellow sugarpaste
- 250 g (9 oz) pink sugarpaste
- 12 edible silver balls
- 1 sheet rice paper

■ UTENSILS

- Carving knife
- 20 cm (8 in) round cake board
- Palette knife
- Rolling pin
- Small sharp knife
- Water and paintbrush
- Pencil
- Scissors

1 Level the top of the cake and place upside-down in the centre of the cake board. Slice and fill the centre with a layer of buttercream and then spread a thin coating of buttercream over the top and sides of the cake.

2 Dust the worksurface with icing sugar. Knead and roll out 250 g (9 oz) of white sugarpaste. Carefully lift the icing over the cake. Smooth the top and sides and neaten the base.

3 Stick one candy stick into the top of the cake to provide internal support for the fairy and roll 50 g (2 oz) of white sugarpaste into an oval shape to form her body. Gently squeeze the centre to make a waist. Lightly moisten a small area on the top of the cake around the protruding candy stick and carefully slot the body into position (*fig 1*).

4 Insert a second candy stick into the top of the body leaving about 3 cm (1¼ in) poking out.

Make a 10 g (¼ oz) ball of flesh-coloured sugarpaste for her head and slot this onto the candy stick. Paint her features using black food colour and a fine paintbrush. You can paint the head before putting it on her body but be careful not to squash the face when lifting it. Add a tiny dot of sugarpaste for a nose.

5 To make her hair, roll 5 g (⅛ oz) of yellow sugarpaste into a strip about 9 cm x 2 cm (3½ in x ¾ in) (*fig 2*). Press lines down the length of the strip using the back of a knife. Stick the strip over her head and tweak the ends upwards to make them look like curls.

For the head-dress make six tiny balls of pink sugarpaste. Stick three in a line on the top of her head with a little water. Stick another two above these and a final one on top.

Finish off her hair by cutting a tiny leaf shape out of some leftover yellow sugarpaste. Press marks into it as you did for the other hair section, then stick this onto the front of her head.

6 Roll out 60 g (2 oz) of pink sugarpaste and cut out a strip approximately 46 cm x 4 cm (18 in x 1½ in). Making sure that the worksurface is well dusted with icing sugar so that the sugarpaste doesn't stick, roll the paintbrush backwards and forwards along a small section of the strip at a time and a wonderful frill will develop (*fig 3*). Paint a line of water just above the base of the cake and, starting from the back of the

holding the fairy wand.

Roll out the leftover yellow sugarpaste and cut out a small star shape. Stick this onto the top of the wand with a little drop of water – not too much or the star will start to slide. You should also find that you are able to rest the star slightly against the fairy's body which will provide it with some additional support.

9 Make a curved row of 12 small dents on the top frill of the fairy's dress using the end of a paintbrush. Put a tiny dab of water in each hollow and then add an edible silver ball as decoration.

10 To make her wings, place the rice paper over the wing template shown on page 109. Trace over it using a pencil. To make the second wing, turn the rice paper over and trace over it the other way. Cut out both wings, cutting just inside the pencil outline to avoid grey edges on the wings.

Take a small lump of white sugarpaste and moisten it with a drop of water so that it becomes slightly tacky. Stick this onto the fairy's back and then carefully insert the two wings. Alternatively, you could stick them into position with a little dab of buttercream.

fairy, carefully stick the frill into place. If it breaks, simply cut off the straggly torn edge and continue with the rest of the frill.

Once you have gone all the way around, repeat the above procedure using about 50 g (1¾ oz) of white sugarpaste to make a white frill. Stick this above the pink so that it overlaps slightly.

Continue up the skirt, alternating pink and white frills right up to the fairy's waist. Each frill will be about 5 cm (2 in) shorter than the last. Try to keep all the joins at the back.

7 Make a ribbon to hide the joins by thinly rolling out 20 g (¾ oz) of pink sugarpaste. Cut out two thin strips for the tails of the ribbon (*fig 3*). Cut a 'V' shape into the end of each one and stick them so that they fall down the back of the skirt.

Top with a 'bow' made of two tiny pink triangles and a small flattened ball of pink for the knot itself. As this detail is not visible from the front of the cake, you could always miss out this stage if you're a bit pushed for time.

8 Press and stick the remaining candy stick against the fairy's body using a little water. This will form the handle of the wand. Roll 10 g (¼ oz) of flesh-coloured sugarpaste into a sausage. Cut this in half for the arms. Flatten one end of each sausage slightly to make her hands, then carefully stick these against the side of the figure to look as though the hands are

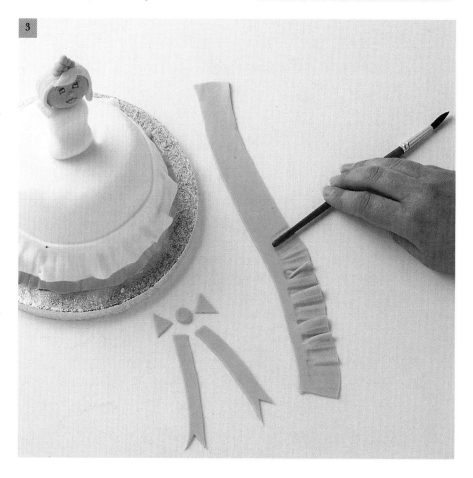

Christmas Santas

Ideal for anyone who loves the nuts and marzipan that abound around Christmas-time, this is an extremely easy cake to decorate. Try to use white marzipan rather than yellow as this takes the colours better.

■ INGREDIENTS

- 20 cm (8 in) round fruit cake (see step 1 before baking.)
- Selection of nuts, such as almonds, pecans, hazelnut, walnuts, etc.
- 45 ml (3 tbsp) brandy (optional)
- 60 ml (4 tbsp) apricot jam
- Icing sugar for rolling out
- Red, paprika, dark brown and green food colour pastes
- 720 g (1 lb 9¼ oz) white (neutral) marzipan, divided and coloured as follows:
  240 g (8¼ oz) red
  150 g (5 oz) flesh colour (paprika)
  120 g (4 oz) dark brown
  30 g (1 oz) green
  Leave the remaining marzipan white (neutral)

■ UTENSILS

- Greaseproof paper
- 23 cm (9 in) round cake board
- Cocktail stick
- Sieve
- Pastry brush
- Rolling pin
- Small sharp knife
- Water and paintbrush

1 Follow the fruit cake recipe for a 20 cm (8 in) round cake on page 95 to the point where you have spooned the mixture into the baking tin. Before placing it in the oven, arrange a selection of nuts over the top of the mixture. Use your favourite nuts or whatever you have in your store-cupboard and start from the outside of the cake and work in. I began with a circle of almonds, then a line of pecans. Next, I added a circle of hazelnuts, some nice big chunky brazil nuts and finally half a walnut in the centre.

Trim a piece of greaseproof paper to fit over the top of the tin and cut a small hole about 3 cm (1¼ in) out of the centre. Rest this over the cake before baking to stop the nuts browning too much during the cooking process. If you have a fan oven, use a sheet of greaseproof long enough to tuck under the baking tin, otherwise it will simply fly off as soon as you shut the door.

Bake as normal, removing the greaseproof about ten minutes before the end of the cooking time just to lightly brown and colour the nuts.

1

2 When the cake has cooled, turn it out of the tin and place onto a 23 cm (9 in) round cake board.

For an extra festive touch, pierce the cake a few times between the nuts with a cocktail stick (you can lift a few up if you wish) and carefully drizzle about 30 ml (2 tbsp) of brandy over the cake. Allow it to seep in and replace any nuts you might have moved.

Boil the apricot jam either in a saucepan or in a non-metallic dish in a microwave for about one minute. Sieve the jam to remove any lumps of fruit and mix in the last remaining tablespoon of brandy. (You may omit the brandy if you prefer.) Paint the mixture over the top and sides of the cake using a pastry brush to give it a wonderfully gleaming finish (fig 1).

3 To make the 12 figures, begin with the bodies. Sprinkle your worksurface with icing sugar. Take a 15 g (½ oz) piece of red-coloured marzipan and roll it into a

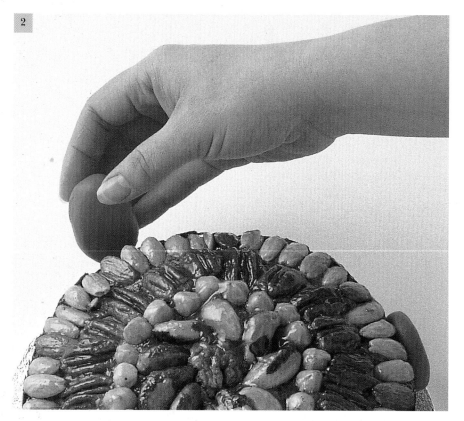

2

flattish conical shape. Press and stick the body up against the side of the cake. You shouldn't need any water to keep it in place – the jam around the sides should be adequate to hold it.

Make another identical body and stick this directly opposite. Stick the third and fourth bodies halfway between the first two (fig 2). The cake should now be divided into quarters. Make and stick another two bodies between each of the four Santas already in position, leaving a small space between each one for his sack. Continue until all the bodies are evenly spaced around the side of the cake.

4   To make a head, roll a 10 g (¼ oz) ball of flesh-coloured marzipan into an oval shape (fig 3). Stick this on top of one of the bodies already in position. Repeat on the other eleven Santas.

5   For each hat, form 5 g (⅛ oz) of red marzipan into a small triangular shape. Tweak the end into a point and bend it over slightly. Place it on one of the heads. The tip of the hat should rest just on top of the cake. Repeat and make hats for all the other figures, ensuring that they all point in the same direction.

6   To make the beards, thinly roll out 10 g (¼ oz) of uncoloured (white) marzipan. Press lines into the marzipan using the

back of a knife and cut out a triangular shape. Stick this onto Santa's face so that the beard hangs over the front of the body. If it won't stay in place, use a little water.

Push the end of a paintbrush into the beard to leave behind a surprised, open-mouthed expression. Stick on a tiny ball of flesh-coloured marzipan for Santa's nose. Repeat on each Santa.

7   To decorate a hat, take about 5 g (⅛ oz) of white marzipan. Pull off a tiny piece and roll it into a ball for the pom-pom. Stick in place. Roll the rest into a sausage and lay it around the brim of the hat so that it almost obscures all the face. Repeat on the rest of the hats.

8   Use 10 g (¼ oz) brown marzipan for each sack and shape into a cone. Stand each one on its fattest part, then pinch and pull the marzipan at the top to make a neck (fig 3). Press one between each Santa on the side of the cake.

9   To make the presents, roll out 30 g (1 oz) green marzipan to a thickness of about 1 cm (⅜ in). Cut out twelve tiny green squares. Using the back of a knife, make a criss-cross pattern on the front of each parcel. Place one in the top of each sack and bend the neck of the sack up slightly. Brush away any dusty icing sugar marks using a damp paintbrush.

TIP

If the marzipan is too hard for you to knead properly, soften it for just a few seconds on high in the microwave.

3

Weary windsurfer

This cake was made for a keen windsurfing friend. If you don't feel up to painting, make the pool from one solid colour or stick spots or other sugarpaste shapes around the sides.

1   Begin by making the surfboard. Roll out 40 g (1 ¾ oz) of white sugarpaste on a surface dusted with icing sugar and cut out a board shape, using the template if necessary. Place the board somewhere out of the way to harden slightly while you assemble the rest of the cake.

2   Level the top of the cake if necessary and turn it upside down. Slice and fill the middle of the cake with buttercream. Reassemble and place the cake in the centre of the cake board. Spread a thin layer of buttercream over the top and sides, saving some if using buttercream for the water.

3   Sprinkle the worksurface with icing sugar and roll out and cover the cake with the rest of the white sugarpaste. Smooth over the top and sides and trim away any excess from the base.

4   Begin constructing the windsurfer by building a life jacket. Shape the orange sugarpaste into a thick cone and press three vertical lines down the length of the

jacket using the back of a knife (*fig 1*). Stick this onto the cake. Roll 20 g (¾ oz) of flesh-coloured sugarpaste into a ball for his head and stick in position. Paint in the eyes using black food colour and a fine paintbrush and stick three tiny balls of flesh-coloured sugarpaste on the face for his ears and nose. To add detail, poke the end of a paintbrush into each ear to leave a little hollow.

5   Take about half a teaspoon of royal icing or buttercream and mix in a little brown food colour. (A nice touch here would be to colour the hair the same shade as the recipient's.) Using a knife, smear the hair on top of the head and pull it up slightly to give it a bit of texture.
   Roll 5 g (⅛ oz) of flesh-coloured sugarpaste into a sausage for one of the arms. Flatten one end slightly to make a hand and stick the arm against the side of the body, bending it at the elbow so that the hand covers the mouth area.

6   For the water, partially mix a little blue food colour into about 30 ml (2 tbsp) of royal icing or buttercream. Spread around the windsurfer on top of the cake (*fig 2*).

7   Roll the dark blue sugarpaste into a sausage about 46 cm (18 in) long. Starting from the back of the cake, lay this around the top edge. Neaten and stick the join together. Place the surfboard in position so that the tip just rests on the edge of the pool. Make two flattish oval shapes from flesh-coloured sugarpaste for his feet and insert these into the water. Make the other arm, squashing one end slightly to make a hand and stick this in place with the palm just resting on the board.

8   Cut a triangle out of thin cardboard and stick this to the candy stick with a little royal icing or buttercream. Insert this into the top of the cake.

INGREDIENTS

- Icing sugar for rolling out
- 300 g (10½ oz) white sugarpaste
- 15 cm (6 in) round cake
- ½ quantity buttercream (see page 98)
- 30 ml (2 tbsp) royal icing (optional)
- 60 g (2 oz) orange sugarpaste
- 50 g (1¾ oz) flesh-coloured sugarpaste
- Assorted food paste colours for painting, including black and brown
- 60 g (2 oz) dark blue sugarpaste
- 1 candy stick (sweet cigarette)
- 30 g (1 oz) green-coloured sugar (see page 98)

UTENSILS

- Rolling pin
- Small sharp knife
- Surfboard template (see page 109)
- Carving knife
- Palette knife
- Water
- Medium and fine paintbrushes
- Thin cardboard triangle for sail
- Clean damp cloth

9   Paint a design on the sides of the pool. Start by painting the colours first and add the outlines in black food colour afterwards. If you do it the other way round, the black will bleed into the colour. If you make a mistake, wash over the area with fresh water and wipe away the mistake with a clean, damp cloth.

10 Moisten the exposed cake board with a little water and carefully spoon the coloured sugar around the base to cover the rest of the board.

Spotty dog

This chap just goes to prove that Man's best friend is his cake! If you're feeling adventurous, why not adapt him to look like the family pet. To make a hairy version, cover him with chocolate buttercream and 'rough it up' with a fork.

■ **INGREDIENTS**

- Icing sugar for rolling out
- 300 g (10½ oz) of green sugarpaste
- 1 pudding basin cake (see page 94)
- 1 quantity buttercream (see page 98)
- 810 g (1 lb 12 oz) white sugarpaste
- 300 g (10½ oz) black sugarpaste
- 20 g (¾ oz) red sugarpaste
- 40 g (1¾ oz) flesh-coloured sugarpaste
- Sweets for decoration

■ **UTENSILS**

- Water and paintbrush
- 30 cm (12 in) round cake board
- Rolling pin
- Carving knife
- Small sharp knife
- Fish slice
- Wooden spoon

1 Begin by covering the cake board. Lightly moisten the board with a little water and place to one side. Sprinkle the worksurface with icing sugar and begin to roll out the green sugarpaste. Carefully lift the icing and place it on the cake board. Continue to roll right to the edges of the cake board. Trim and neaten the edges and place the board to one side again.

2 On a spare cake board, cutting board or worksurface, check the cake will lie flat when it is turned upside down. Slice a little off the base if necessary. Cut the cake in half, and fill the middle with a layer of buttercream. Spread a thin coating of buttercream around the sides and top of the cake as well.

   Knead and roll out 300 g (10½ oz) of white sugarpaste. Lift and place the icing over the cake and carefully smooth it into position. Trim and neaten around the base. Lift the cake using a fish slice to help avoid getting fingerprints in the icing and place it towards the back of the covered cake board.

3 To make the dog's head, take 200 g (7 oz) of white sugarpaste and roll this into a ball. Flatten the ball slightly into a thick disc about 11 cm (4½ in) wide and stick this to the front of the cake.

4 To make the dog's eyes, thinly roll out about 20 g (¾ oz) of black sugarpaste. Cut out two discs about 4.5 cm (1¾ in) wide and two about 2.5 cm (1 in) in diameter.

   Wipe your hands (black sugarpaste has an annoying tendency to get everywhere!) and roll out about 10 g (¼ oz) of white sugarpaste. Cut out two discs each about 3 cm (1¼ in) wide and squash two tiny balls of white to make the tiny discs for the highlights. Assemble and stick the eyes in position on the face starting with the largest black disc first and alternating the colours.

5 For the tongue, use 20 g (¾ oz) of red sugarpaste. Roll this into a sort of flattish, carrot shape and bend it into a slight curve. Press a line down the centre using the back of a knife and stick it into position on the board, the pointed end just touching the base of the face.

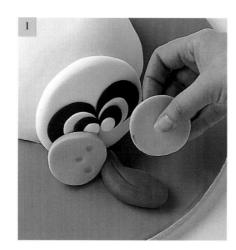

6 To make the dog's muzzle, divide the flesh-coloured sugarpaste in two and roll each half into a ball. Flatten each ball into a disc about 5 cm (2 in) in diameter. Stick the two circles in place and make three small dents in each using the end of a wooden spoon (fig 1).

   Finish off the face by sticking a small ball of black sugarpaste onto the muzzle for his nose.

7 To make the legs, divide 300 g (10½ oz) of white sugarpaste into four. Roll each quarter into a chunky carrot shape. Flatten each paw slightly and stick them on the board around the dog. Using the back of a knife, press three short lines into the front of each paw.

8 To make the ears, take 150 g (5 oz) of black sugarpaste. Divide it into two pieces and roll each half into the same sort of carrot shape as you did for the legs.

Use a rolling pin to flatten each half into an ear shape. Stick one either side of the head (fig 2).

9 Roll out 100 g (3½ oz) of black sugarpaste and cut out 'splodges' in a variety of shapes and sizes. Stick these all over the dog's back. Make a tail by rolling 10 g (¼ oz) of black sugarpaste into a tapering sausage shape. Bend it into a curl and stick in position.

10 Decorate the cake board with a selection of small sweets, securing them in place with little dabs of buttercream.

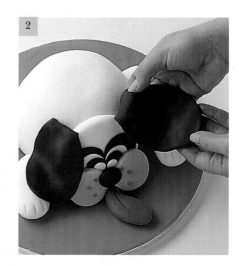

Football fan

Although the theme of this cake is football, it could be adapted to suit other sports too. Substitute a brown sugarpaste oval for the football and you have a rugby cake. Dress him in white with a bat and it becomes a cricket cake.

1 Slice a little off the top of the cake to level it if necessary. Turn it upside down and place towards the back of the board. Slice and fill the middle of the cake with buttercream, then reassemble and spread a thin covering of buttercream over the top and sides.

2 Dust the worksurface with a little icing sugar and knead all the green sugarpaste until pliable. Roll it out, then lift and place over the cake. Smooth over the top and sides, preferably with a cake smoother, as this irons out any lumps and bumps. Alternatively, simply smooth it as best you can with the flat of your hand. Trim away any excess from around the base.

3 Make the scarf by rolling out 250 g (8 oz) of the white sugarpaste and cutting it into a strip 30 cm x 10 cm (12 in x 4 in). Moisten the top of the cake and carefully lay the scarf over the top. Roll out and cut 150 g (5 oz) of red sugarpaste into about seven thin strips about 3 cm x 10 cm (1½ in x 4 in). Lay and stick the red stripes across the scarf. When you come to the ones at either end, cut a fringe into the strip before laying it into position on the board (*fig 1*).

4 Begin with the footballer's feet. Divide the black sugarpaste in two and roll each half into an oval. Stick these onto the board in front of the cake. Make two socks by

INGREDIENTS

- 15 cm (6 in) square sponge cake
- 1 quantity buttercream (see page 98)
- Icing sugar for rolling out
- 350 g (12 oz) green sugarpaste
- 300 g (10½ oz) white sugarpaste
- 150 g (5 oz) red sugarpaste
- 20 g (¾ oz) black sugarpaste
- 30 g (1 oz) flesh-coloured sugarpaste
- 40 g (1¾ oz) blue sugarpaste
- Black food colour
- 5 g (⅛ oz) brown sugarpaste
- 60 g (2 oz) green-coloured coconut (see page 98)

UTENSILS

- Carving knife
- 25 cm (10 in) square cake board
- Palette knife
- Cake smoother (optional)
- Small sharp knife
- Water
- Medium and fine paintbrushes

1

rolling 10 g (¼ oz) of white sugarpaste into two balls. Flatten each ball slightly and press a few horizontal lines into each sock with the back of a knife. Stick these onto the boots (*fig 2*).

  Make the footballer's legs by rolling 10 g (¼ oz) of flesh-coloured sugarpaste into a thin string. Cut this in half and stick into position.

5 For his shorts, take 10 g (¼ oz) of white sugarpaste and roll it into a boomerang shape (*fig 3*). Stick on top of the cake. Pull off and keep a little bit of the blue sugarpaste to make the sleeves later. Roll the rest into a cone for his body and stick

TIP

If the footballer loses his head or falls over, insert a small strand of dried spaghetti inside the body and slot the head on top for extra support.

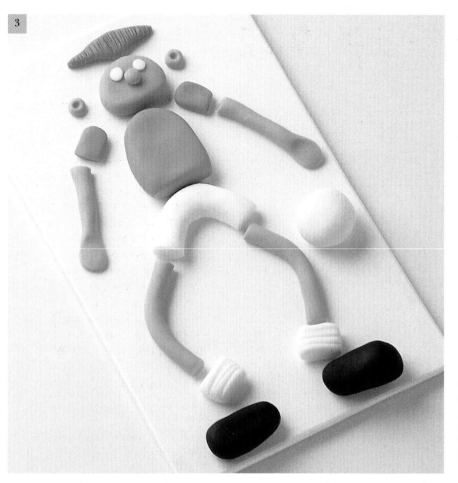

making a small dent in them with the end of a paintbrush.

Paint in the pupils, eyebrows and mouth with black food colour. Finally, roll a little brown sugarpaste into a tiny strip and place on top of the head. Press some lines into the hair with the back of a knife.

9 Moisten the top of the cake and any exposed cake board with a little water and then sprinkle with the green-coloured coconut to look like the grass of a football pitch.

> **TIP**
> *If you know the home colours of the recipient's favourite football team, make the scarf and the footballer's kit in the appropriate shades.*

on top of the shorts *(fig 3)*. Flatten the top of the cone slightly so the head has a level surface to sit on.

6 For the football, roll 20 g (¾ oz) of white sugarpaste into a ball. Stick this in place and paint a hexagonal design on the front with black food colour and a fine paintbrush. (If you don't want to paint, just press a few lines into the ball with the back of a knife or leave it plain.)

7 Roll 5 g (⅛ oz) of flesh-coloured sugarpaste into a thin sausage to make his arms. Cut in two and flatten one end of each half to make the hands. Stick these into position.

Make two tiny shirt sleeves by rolling the leftover blue sugarpaste into an oval. Cut in half and stick one on the top of each arm.

8 To make the head, roll 10 g (¼ oz) of flesh-coloured sugarpaste into a ball. Stick on top of the body.

Stick two tiny flattened discs of white sugarpaste onto the face for his eyes and three small balls of flesh-coloured sugarpaste in position for his ears and nose. Add some detail to the ears by

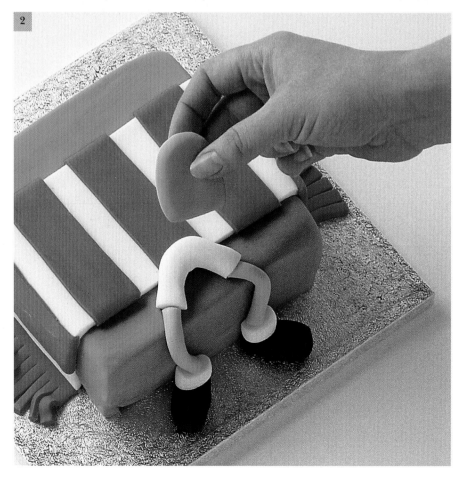

Make-up bag

This is for anyone who likes to experiment with the latest cosmetics. It is also very adaptable. Make a brown bag and fill with icing toys for a Christmas sack or pack with icing pencils and books for a 'Back to School' cake.

INGREDIENTS

- Icing sugar for rolling out
- 60 g (2 oz) grey sugarpaste
- 30 g (1 oz) dark brown sugarpaste
- 20 g (¾ oz) flesh-coloured sugarpaste
- 60 g (2 oz) light brown sugarpaste
- 120 g (4¼ oz) black sugarpaste
- 20 g (¾ oz) dark blue sugarpaste
- 10 g (¼ oz) light blue sugarpaste
- 700 g (1 lb 9 oz) white sugarpaste
- 20 g (¾ oz) red sugarpaste
- 130 g (4¼ oz) pink sugarpaste
- 10 g (¼ oz) pale green sugarpaste
- 15 cm (6 in) round sponge cake
- ½ quantity buttercream (see page 98)

UTENSILS

- Rolling pin
- Small sharp knife
- Water and paintbrush
- Carving knife
- Palette knife
- 23 cm (9 in) round cake board
- Ruler

1 Begin by making up the little cosmetics themselves *(fig 1)* and, if possible, leave them overnight to harden. This will give them the strength to stand up and look even more realistic. If the recipient has a particular penchant for any specific brand of make-up or perfume, it might be fun to try to copy the bottles or packaging to give the cake a really personal touch.

Dust the worksurface with icing sugar. To make a basic eyeshadow palette, roll out about 20 g (¾ oz) of grey sugarpaste. Roll it fairly thickly and cut out a semi-circle. Roll out three small lumps of sugarpaste in various shades of brown and paprika and cut a different section of a smaller semi-circle out of each. Stick these onto the grey.

2 To make a duo eyeshadow, roll and cut about 10 g (¼ oz) of black sugarpaste into a rectangle. Cut two smaller rectangles out of two different shades of blue sugarpaste and stick these onto the black. Make an applicator wand by rolling a little light brown sugarpaste into a thin string and sticking a tiny oval of white or cream sugarpaste on either end.

3 To make a lipstick, roll about 10 g (¼ oz) of grey sugarpaste into a thick sausage. Slice a little off both ends to neaten them and press two lines across the icing using the back of a knife. Make another smaller sausage out of pink, red or whatever shade of sugarpaste you like and slice a small section to flatten one of the ends. Make a diagonal cut through the other end to make an authentic lipstick shape and stick the two sections together. Make another two or three of these.

To make a lip pencil, roll about 10 g (¼ oz) of red sugarpaste into a sausage about 9 cm (3 ½ in) long. Slice a little off both ends to neaten them. Roll a small piece of flesh-coloured sugarpaste into a tiny cone and slice a little off the pointed end. Make a tiny red point and stick all three sections together. Make a couple of eye pencils in exactly the same way using blue and brown sugarpaste.

4 For the blusher brush, roll about 20 g (¾ oz) of light brown sugarpaste into a sausage. Slice off both ends to neaten them. Roll a little grey sugarpaste into a ball. Flatten the ball slightly and stick this against the brown. Press two lines into the grey with the back of a knife to add detail.

Roll out about 10 g (¼ oz) of black sugarpaste to a thickness of about 1 cm (⅜ in). Cut this into a triangular shape with a flat top and make bristles by pressing lines down the length of the shape with a knife. Stick the 'brush' in place on the handle.

1

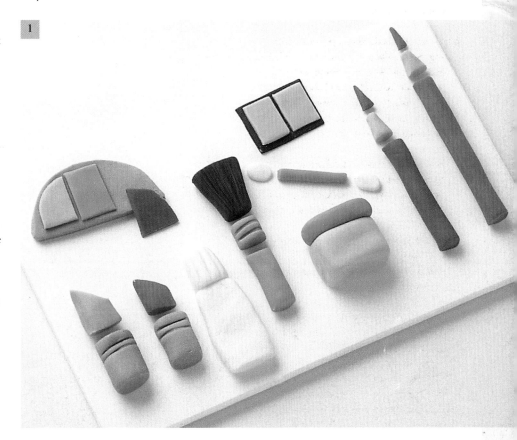

5 Make a simple pot of cream by rolling about 60 g (2 oz) of white sugarpaste into a round cylindrical shape with a flat base and top. Roll 20 g (¾ oz) of pink sugarpaste into a thick disc and stick this on top of the pot. Press a few vertical lines around the edge of the lid. Make another smaller pot out of two shades of brown sugarpaste to sit on the board.

6 To make a tube, roll about 20 g (¾ oz) of white sugarpaste into a slightly tapering rectangular shape. Make a small flowerpot shape out of a little white sugarpaste and stick this onto the end of the tube for a lid. Press lines down the length of the lid using the back of a knife.

7 For the mascara wand, simply roll about 10 g (¼ oz) of pale green sugarpaste into a sausage. Neaten both ends and press two lines into the icing about a third of the way along the top of the shape. Make any additional cosmetics and place all the components to one side whilst you deal with the cake.

8 Slice and fill the middle of the cake with buttercream. Reassemble the cake and place it in the centre of the board. Spread a thin covering of buttercream over the top and sides.

  Roll out 100 g (3½ oz) of black sugarpaste and cut out a 15 cm (6 in) disc and place on top of the cake. You could use your baking tin as a template for this but accuracy is not vitally important here as most of it will be hidden. The reason for the black is simply to help seal in the cake beneath and to give the illusion that the bag is full, should you have any gaps between your components. Place the pink and white pot and the white tube of cream on top of the black.

9 Take 300 g (10½ oz) of white sugarpaste and 100 g (3½ oz) of pink. Partially knead

> **TIP**
> *For a really quick cake with no modelling, simply fill the top of the cake with sweets or biscuits instead.*

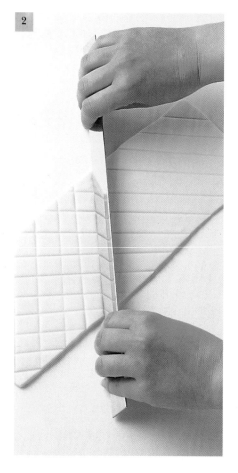

the two colours together to achieve a light marbled effect. Roll the icing out fairly thickly and cut out a strip about 46 cm x 15 cm (18 in x 6 in). Using the edge of a clean ruler, gently press a criss-cross pattern across the strip to give a quilted effect (*fig 2*).

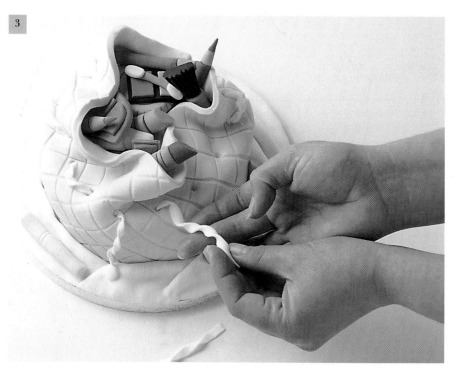

10 Carefully wind the strip up loosely like a bandage and, holding it vertically, start at the back and unwind it around the side of the cake (see page 38). Neaten the join and base. If it looks a bit flat in places, insert a few lumps of sugarpaste to pad out the top of the bag slightly. Using the end of a paintbrush, make a line of circular dents around the side of the bag. Carefully place the cosmetics into the top of the bag and secure with a little water.

11 Moisten the exposed cake board. Thinly roll out 250 g (9 oz) of white sugarpaste into a long strip. Lay the strip around the base of the cake allowing it to fall into folds like fabric. Press down the icing at the edges of the board and trim away any excess. Place any leftover cosmetics around the board.

12 Thinly roll out 20 g (¾ oz) of white sugarpaste and cut into small thin strips. Take one strip and twist it (*fig 3*). Hang it between two of the holes around the side of the cake and secure the ends with a little water. Repeat using alternate holes to look like a cord threaded through the icing. When you come to the final two at the front of the cake, allow them to hang down. Finish off each one with a tiny ball of white sugarpaste.

Lovebirds

Here's a novel idea for an engagement cake without a pink sugar heart in sight! It would also make a loving gift for Valentine's day. This is an extremely easy cake to put together as the chocolate sticks hide a multitude of sins!

■ INGREDIENTS

- Icing sugar for rolling out
- 120 g (4 oz) pale blue sugarpaste
- 10 g (¼ oz) white sugarpaste
- Black food colour
- 1 pudding bowl cake (see page 94)
- ½ quantity chocolate buttercream (see page 98)
- Two 120 g (4 oz) boxes of chocolate sticks (flavour of your choice!)
- 60 g (2 oz) dark blue sugarpaste
- 30 g (1 oz) green sugarpaste

■ UTENSILS

- Water
- Fine and medium paintbrushes
- Rolling pin
- Piping nozzle
- Small sharp knife
- Carving knife
- 20 cm (8 in) round cake board
- Palette knife
- Template for tail (see page 109)
- Garrett frill or jam tart cutter

1 Roll two 60 g (2 oz) lumps of pale blue sugarpaste into two conical shapes for the birds' bodies. Check that the bases are flat enough for them to stand upright. Make two 30 g (1 oz) balls of pale blue sugarpaste for the heads (*fig 1*). Stick a head onto each body with a little water.

2 To make the eyes, thinly roll out about 10 g (¼ oz) of white sugarpaste. Cut out four small circles using a piping nozzle and stick two on each head. Paint pupils and eyelashes using black food colour. Make two tiny yellow sugarpaste triangles for the beaks. Press a line using the back of a knife into the sides of each beak and stick one on each bird. Make a tiny pale blue triangle and press a few lines into the front of it. Stick it on top of the male bird's head. Put the birds to one side.

3 Level the top of the cake if necessary and slice and fill the centre with buttercream. Reassemble the cake and dab a little buttercream in the centre of the cake board to help hold the cake in place.

Stand the cake, widest part up, and spread a thick layer of buttercream all over the sides and top.

4 Place the two birds into position on top of the cake and begin to build up the nest. Do this by pressing the chocolate sticks, one at a time, around the sides of the nest (*fig 2*) and over the top edge.

5 Roll out 30 g (1 oz) of the dark blue sugarpaste and cut out a tail using the template on page 109 if necessary. Re-knead the leftover icing and cut out a second tail. Place the two tails in position, one behind each bird.

6 To make the birds' wings, roll out another 30 g (1 oz) of dark blue sugarpaste and using either a garrett frill or a jam tart cutter, cut out a frilly circle. Re-knead the sugarpaste and cut out a second circle of the same size. Cut both circles in half. Carefully stick two wings onto each of the birds, overlapping them slightly at the front as though they are holding hands (sorry – wings!) (*fig 3*).

7 Roll out the green sugarpaste and cut out some simple leaves. Press a couple of veins into each leaf using the back of a knife and stick the leaves around the board and against the cake with a little water.

Woodland creatures

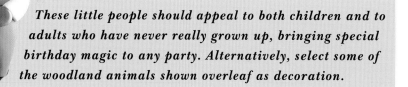

These little people should appeal to both children and to adults who have never really grown up, bringing special birthday magic to any party. Alternatively, select some of the woodland animals shown overleaf as decoration.

INGREDIENTS

- 18 cm (7 in) round sponge cake
- 1 quantity buttercream (see page 98)
- Icing sugar for rolling out
- 800 g (1 lb 12 oz) white marzipan
- Dark brown food colour paste
- 200 g (7 oz) white sugarpaste
- 50 g (2 oz) flesh-coloured sugarpaste
- 100 g (4 oz) mint green sugarpaste
- 50 g (2 oz) gooseberry green sugarpaste
- 50 g (2 oz) red sugarpaste
- 20 g (¾ oz) black sugarpaste
- 10 g (¼ oz) grey sugarpaste
- Black food colour paste
- 75 g (3 oz) dark brown sugar

UTENSILS

- 28 cm (11 in) round cake board
- Carving knife
- Palette knife
- Rolling pin
- 18 cm (7 in) round cake board or plate
- Small sharp knife
- Water
- Paintbrush

1 Level the top of the cake and turn it upside down. Slice the cake in two and fill the centre with buttercream. Place on the board and spread more buttercream around the sides and top.

2 Knead and roll out 300 g (11 oz) of the white marzipan. Place either an 18 cm (7 in) round cake board or plate on top to act as a template and cut round it using a sharp knife. Place the marzipan disc on top of the cake.

3 Roll out the remaining marzipan and cut a strip measuring approximately 58 cm x 8 cm (23 in x 3 in). Carefully roll up the strip like a bandage then unwind it around the side of the cake (*fig 1*).

4 Press irregular vertical lines around the sides of the cake using the back of a knife.

TIP

Use the leaves as camouflage and position them to hide any mistakes or unsightly marks!

Use a paintbrush to paint the bark with a wash of watered-down brown food colour (*fig 2*). Finally, paint a few 'age' rings on top of the tree stump with brown food colour and a fine paintbrush.

5 To make the troll, roll out 30 g (1 oz) of white sugarpaste into a cone (*fig 3*) to form the basis for his body. Stick this in position on top of the tree stump.

6 For the troll's legs, roll 20 g (¾ oz) of mint green sugarpaste into a sausage and cut this in half. Stick the two halves to the base of the body.

7 To make the arms, roll 10 g (¼ oz) of white sugarpaste into a sausage and cut in half, as for the legs. Stick one arm either side of the body.

11 For each toadstool, roll out 10 g (¼ oz) of white sugarpaste into a cone (*fig 4*). Make another three cones and stick them in position around the base of the cake. Divide 20 g (1 oz) of the red sugarpaste into two and roll into little balls. Cut each ball in half and stick one on top of each toadstool base. Decorate each one with a few tiny flattened discs of white sugarpaste.

12 To make the snail, roll 10 g (¼ oz) of grey sugarpaste into a small sausage. Paint a line of water along the top. Roll it up, leaving about 2 cm (¾ in) protruding for the head (*fig 4*).

Pinch two tiny 'feelers' out of the top of the head and paint three dots of black food colour on the face for the eyes and mouth. Place the snail at the foot of the tree stump and secure with a little water.

13 For the leaves, take the two remaining shades of green coloured sugarpaste and roll each one out flat. Cut out some very

dots of black food colour on the face for his eyes.

10 Repeat steps 5-9 given above for the remaining trolls, although you can omit making legs for the one shown on the right of the cake as his lower body is strategically hidden by some of the leaves!

TIP

If your marzipan is difficult to handle, soften it for a few seconds on high in the microwave.

8 Stick a small ball of flesh-coloured sugarpaste on top of the body for the troll's head. For the hat, roll 10 g (¼ oz) of red sugarpaste into a pointed triangular shape and stick on top of the head, tweaking the end out at an angle. Make three tiny balls of flesh-coloured sugarpaste. Use one for his nose and the other two as hands. Make two tiny flesh-coloured triangles for ears. Stick these in place and add a little detail by pressing the end of a paintbrush lightly into each ear.

9 To complete the troll, make two small ovals of black sugarpaste and stick one onto the end of each leg. Paint two tiny

basic leaf shapes using the tip of a knife. Press a simple vein pattern into each leaf using the back of the knife *(fig 5)*. Arrange around the scene.

14 Lightly moisten the exposed cake board and carefully spoon the dark brown sugar around the bottom of the cake board to look like earth.

TIP

Instead of sugar, you could substitute green-coloured desiccated coconut as grass. Together with quick-to-make details like the little snail, the area around the cake contributes to the overall 'tableau' resulting in a totally professional finish.

Decorating variation

In this alternative version, I have used rabbits instead of figures. Instructions for making these appear on page 105 and the effect is just as charming as the original. Add some sugar eggs for an Easter theme. If your creativity is really flowing, you could also add mice, squirrels or other small creatures. You could also devise a Christmas or winter scene. Spread a layer of royal icing over the top of the tree stump and the group to look like snow and add beards and white trims to the hats of the figures.

Santa and his teddies

I do like cakes that tell a story. It means that people actually have to take some time to look at them to work out what's going on. Here, Santa and his helper are putting the finishing touches to some teddies ready for the big night.

1 Although I have used a traditional fruit cake base here, you could substitute sponge if you prefer. Just omit the brandy, jam and marzipan and use buttercream instead. To shape the cake, cut irregular lumps out of the cake and place these pieces around the cake to create the snow drifts *(fig 1)*. (You could leave the cake intact if you prefer.)

   If you wish, pierce the cake a few times with a cocktail stick and drizzle the brandy over the top. Place the cake on the board and 'paint' with boiled apricot jam, applied with a pastry brush.

2 Dust the worksurface with icing sugar and knead the marzipan until pliable. (If it is difficult to knead, heat it for a few seconds in a microwave on full power.) Roll it out and cover the cake.

3 Lightly moisten the whole of the cake and the exposed cake board with a little water. Roll out 400 g (14 oz) of white sugarpaste. Lay this over the cake and board. Smooth the icing over the cake and board, starting from the centre to try to prevent air bubbles from forming in the hollows. Trim and neaten the edges.

   If you do get an air bubble, prick it gently with the cocktail stick and press out. Hide the little hole left by the cocktail stick under a figure or snowball later.

4 To make Santa, roll 40 g (1¼ oz) of red sugarpaste into a cone *(fig 2)*. Stick this in

INGREDIENTS

- 15 cm (6 in) square fruit cake
- 45 ml (3 tbsp) brandy (optional)
- 45 ml (3 tbsp) boiled apricot jam
- Icing sugar for rolling out
- 500 g (1 lb 2 oz) marzipan
- 450 g (1 lb) white sugarpaste
- 50 g (2 oz) red sugarpaste
- 30 g (1 oz) flesh-coloured sugarpaste
- Black food colour
- 30 g (1 oz) golden brown sugarpaste
- 30 g (1 oz) green sugarpaste

UTENSILS

- Carving knife
- Cocktail stick
- 20 cm (8 in) square cake board
- Pastry brush
- Rolling pin
- Small sharp knife
- Water
- Medium and fine paintbrushes
- Drinking straw

1

the middle of the cake. Roll 10 g (¼ oz) of flesh-coloured sugarpaste into a ball for his head and stick on the body.

   To make his beard, roll out about 5 g (⅛ oz) of white sugarpaste and cut out a triangular shape. Press lines into the beard with the back of a knife and stick onto the face. Stick a tiny ball of flesh-coloured sugarpaste just above the beard for his nose and two either side of the head for his ears. Push the end of a paintbrush into each ear to add detail.

   For the hat, roll 5 g (⅛ oz) of red sugarpaste into a triangle. Stick on top of the head and bend the end over slightly. Roll 5 g (⅛ oz) of white sugarpaste into a thin sausage and lay this around the base of the hat. Stick a small ball of white on the end of the hat for a pom-pom. Paint two dots of black food colour for his eyes.

5 Next, roll 10 g (¼ oz) of black sugarpaste into a sausage about 7.5 cm (3 in) long for his boots. Cut this in half and bend up the end of each to make an 'L' shape. Stick in position, making sure that you leave enough room for the teddy later. Press a few lines into the sole of each boot with the

give each a glum-looking mouth by pressing a drinking straw held at an angle to leave an upside-down, semi-circular impression. Paint the pupils on these teddies as though they are looking to the right.

On the finished teddies add ears, and pupils looking to the left. Hold and press the drinking straw the other way up to give them smiling expressions.

8   To make the elf's body, roll 10 g (¼ oz) of green sugarpaste into a ball (fig 3). Stick towards the front of the cake. Roll 5 g (⅛ oz) of flesh-coloured sugarpaste into a ball for his head and stick on the body.

Top the head with a small triangle of green and tweak the end into position.

Make eyes in the same way as for the teddies and paint a smiling mouth using black food colour. Make two tiny pointed ears and a nose and stick in position on the head.

To make the legs, roll 5 g (⅛ oz) of green sugarpaste into a sausage. Cut in half and stick in position. Make a smaller sausage for the arms and stick these in place too. Make two tiny flesh-coloured hands and make and place a teddy's ear in one. Stick in place.

Make two smaller versions of Santa's boots out of 5 g (⅛ oz) of black sugarpaste and stick on the ends of the legs. Finally, roll any leftover bits of white sugarpaste into balls and stick around the cake to look like snowballs.

TIP

If you are very short of time, just make the one teddy that Santa is in the process of finishing off – the cake will look just as charming and will take you far less time. You could also leave out Santa's helper if you wish.

back of a knife. Roll 10 g (¼ oz) of white sugarpaste into a sausage about 17 cm (7 in) long. Lay this neatly around the base of the figure.

6   Make the first teddy. Roll 10 g (¼ oz) of the brown sugarpaste into a cone (fig 3). Stick this in front of Santa. Roll 5 g (⅛ oz) of brown sugarpaste into a ball for his head. Stick this on top of the body. Make two small sausage shapes for his legs and bend up the end of each one to make a foot. Stick one either side of the body. Stick two smaller sausage shapes in place for his arms.

Make two tiny flattened white sugarpaste discs for his eyes and one black one for a nose and stick in position. Paint in the pupils with black food colour. Stick a small ball of brown on top of the head for an ear and add detail with the end of a paintbrush.

Roll 5 g (⅛ oz) of red sugarpaste into a sausage. Cut this in half to make Santa's arms and stick these in position on his body. Make two tiny flesh-coloured oval shapes for his hands and stick these on the ends of the arms.

7   Make another five teddies in the same way (you will probably find it easier to make these away from the cake and to stick them in position when they are finished). On the three unfinished teddies, omit the ears and

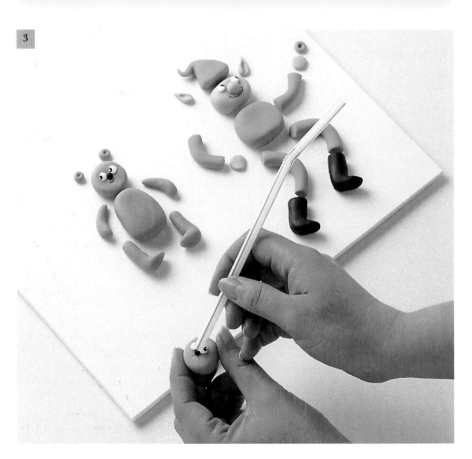

3

Comfy chair

Unless they have a hobby, men can be difficult subjects to make cakes for. This is a neat solution, ideal for a birthday or Father's Day. If it's children that harangue him rather than a cat, substitute a child climbing over the back instead.

■ INGREDIENTS

- Icing sugar for rolling out
- 160 g (5½ oz) white sugarpaste
- 15 cm (6 in) round sponge cake
- ½ quantity buttercream (see page 98)
- 350 g (12½ oz) pale blue sugarpaste
- 80 g (2¾ oz) grey sugarpaste
- 20 g (¾ oz) black sugarpaste
- 80 g (2¾ oz) green sugarpaste
- 30 g (1 oz) flesh-coloured sugarpaste
- Black food colour
- 10 g (¼ oz) brown sugarpaste

■ UTENSILS

- 20 cm (8 in) round cake board
- Water and paintbrush
- Rolling pin
- Small sharp knife
- Carving knife
- Fish slice (optional)
- Palette knife
- Cocktail stick (optional)
- Drinking straw

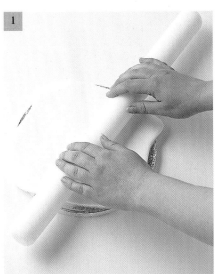

1 Cover the board with white sugarpaste as on page 100. Trim away the excess and place the board to one side (*fig 1*).

2 Cut the cake into shape by slicing off about one third. Place the smaller, cutaway piece flat side down on the remaining section of cake to form the basic seat shape (*fig 2*). If there is not much seat area, slice a thin section away from the back of the chair. 'Glue' the two sections of seat together with buttercream. Spread a layer of buttercream over the outside of the cake.

3 Knead and roll out 300 g (10½ oz) of pale blue sugarpaste. Carefully lift up the icing and place over the cake. To prevent air being trapped, start from the central seat area and smooth the icing into position. You may find that the icing gathers into folds at the back of the chair. These can usually be eased out by gently lifting and fanning the icing out slightly. Trim and neaten the base.

4 Carefully lift and place the cake towards the back of the covered cake board. If you're worried about getting fingerprints in the icing, use a fish slice to lift it.

5 Roll out about 50 g (2 oz) of the pale blue sugarpaste. Cut out a strip about 46 cm x 3 cm (18 in x 1¼ in). Ideally the strip should be slightly wavy down one of the longest sides. This is not essential but it does make for a better frill. Making sure you have plenty of icing sugar on the worksurface to prevent the frill sticking, roll a paintbrush or cocktail stick backwards and forwards over the wavy edge of the strip (*fig 3*). Paint a line of water around the side of the cake, about 3 cm (1¼ in) up from the base. Stick the frill around the cake. Neaten the join by pushing the end of a paintbrush along the top of the strip to leave a circular pattern.

6 To make the cushions, roll out about 60 g (2 oz) of white sugarpaste fairly thickly. Cut out three squares about 6 cm (2½ in) square. Tweak the ends slightly and using the end of a drinking straw, poke four small circles into each one to look like buttons (*fig 4*). Stick the cushions onto the back of the chair.

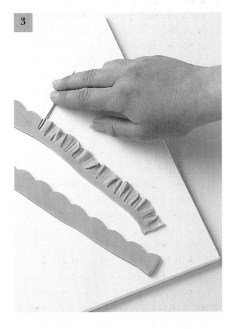

7 To make the man himself, begin with his legs. Roll 80 g (2¾ oz) of grey sugarpaste into a long sausage. Cut the sausage in half and stick it onto the chair. Roll two 10 g (¼ oz) lumps of black sugarpaste into oval shapes for his feet and stick one on the end of each leg.

Decorating variation

A comfy chair is not just for people to snooze in — in fact, once you have made the basic shape you could sit virtually anything on it. The cat in this variation looks especially at home! Make a potato like those in the flowerpot cake (page 68), decorate it with eyes and a mouth, sit it on the seat and you have a cheeky couch-potato cake. A chair cake is an extremely useful shape to add to your repertoire because it provides an easy way to put full-length, upright figures onto a cake without having to fiddle about with awkward supports inside them.

as I did, that the head flops backwards, simply prop it up with a small triangle of white sugarpaste which will just look like another cushion. Push the end of a paintbrush into the lower part of the head and pull it down slightly to give him an open-mouthed expression.

Stick a small ball of sugarpaste on the front of the face for his nose and two at the sides for his ears. Add a little detail to the ears by making a small hollow with the end of a paintbrush. Either paint in the eyes with black food colour or press two semi-circular impressions into the face using the drinking straw held at an angle.

Add two flattened balls of flesh-coloured sugarpaste for his hands.

10 To make the newspaper, cut a flat rectangle out of 10 g (¼ oz) of white sugarpaste. Fold the icing in half, then half again. Paint squiggles onto the newspaper with black food colour to resemble the print and stick the paper onto the man's lap.

11 To make the cat, roll about 5 g (⅛ oz) of brown sugarpaste into a tapering sausage shape for his body. Pinch a couple of small ears out of the thicker end.

Stick two tiny strings of brown sugarpaste onto the back of the chair for his paws and stick the body on top. Roll another tiny piece of sugarpaste into a string for his tail. Paint on the cat's features and stripes neatly with some black food colour.

8 Make his body by rolling 50 g (2 oz) of green sugarpaste into a conical shape and stick this on top of the legs (fig 5). Roll out a thin strip of the same colour green and press vertical lines into the strip using the back of your knife. Lay this around the base of his jumper. Make a polo neck by sticking a small but thick disc of green sugarpaste on top of the jumper and again press a few vertical lines around the edge.

For his arms, roll 20 g (¾ oz) of the green sugarpaste into a sausage. Cut it in half and arrange and stick the arms in whatever position you wish.

9 To make the man's head, roll 20 g (¾ oz) of flesh-coloured sugarpaste into a ball (fig 6). Stick this onto the neck. If you find,

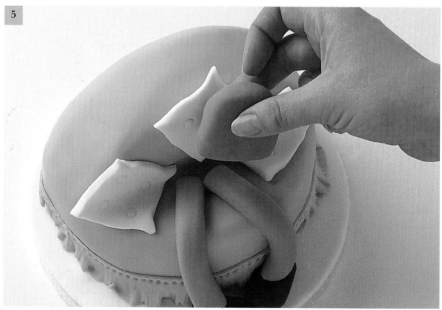

Piggy bank

Here's a cake to appeal to anyone with an interest in money, from the youngest saver to the most hard-bitten of accountants. To make the pig more dramatic, paint a pattern on his back using food colours or stick on sugarpaste shapes.

■ INGREDIENTS

- Icing sugar for rolling out
- 200 g (7 oz) green sugarpaste
- Cake baked in a pudding basin (see page 94)
- ½ quantity buttercream (see page 98)
- 340 g (12 oz) pink sugarpaste
- 10 g (¼ oz) white sugarpaste
- 20 g (¾ oz) black sugarpaste
- About 200 g (7 oz), or 4 small bags, of chocolate coins
- 15 ml (1 tbsp) royal icing (optional)

■ UTENSILS

- 25 cm (10 in) round cake board
- Water and paintbrush
- Rolling pin
- Small sharp knife
- Icing nozzle
- Drinking straw
- Wooden spoon
- Large circle cutter (optional)

1 Cover the cake board with green sugarpaste as explained on page 100. Trim and neaten the edges, then place the covered board to one side.

2 Slice and fill the centre of the cake with buttercream. Reassemble the cake and spread a layer of buttercream over the top and sides. Roll out and cover the cake with 250 g (8¾ oz) of pink sugarpaste. Trim and neaten the base, then place the cake towards the rear of the covered cake board.

3 Make a simple floral pattern on the pig's back by pressing something circular (such as an icing nozzle or small circle cutter) into the icing while it is still pliable, then surrounding it with smaller circles made from a drinking straw (fig 1).

4 To make his face (fig 2), thinly roll out 10 g (¼ oz) of white sugarpaste. Cut out two discs about 2.5 cm (1 in) in diameter. Stick these to the front of the pig. Roll out the black sugarpaste and cut out two smaller discs and a small rectangle for the money slot. Stick the circles onto his eyes and the slot in the middle of his back. Finish off each eye with a tiny flattened ball of white sugarpaste as a highlight.

5 For his snout, roll and shape 40 g (1¾ oz) of pink sugarpaste into a thick disc about 6.5 cm (2½ in) in diameter. Stick this to the front of his face. Don't use too much

water to do this or the snout will start to slide. Using the end of a wooden spoon, press two nostrils into the snout. Make a mouth either by pressing something circular into the icing (such as a cutter) or by using the back of a knife to make a curved line. Make two small cuts at each end of the mouth.

6 Make a tail by rolling about 5 g (⅛ oz) of pink sugarpaste into a tapering sausage shape. Bend it into a curly tail shape and stick to the back of the pig.

7 To make the pig's ears, roll out 40 g (1¾ oz) of pink sugarpaste to a thickness of about 5 mm (¼ in). Cut out an ear shape, using the template if necessary. Scrunch up the leftover icing and cut out a second ear. Stick the ears to the sides of the head, allowing them to fold over slightly at the top (fig 3).

8 Cut one of the chocolate coins in half and press it into the money slot. A drop of water should be enough to hold it in place but you could use a dab of royal icing if you prefer. Arrange the rest of the coins around the board.

TIP

If you don't have any royal icing readily available for sticking the coins, use leftover buttercream instead. It will hold them in place just as well, but may be a little greasy when unwrapping the coins.

Christening cake

If you're worried about piping directly onto the top of this cake, two methods of writing in icing are also shown. Read the instructions in step 1 first and see which one suits you best.

■ INGREDIENTS

*   Royal icing (see page 99)
*   20 cm (8 in) round sponge cake
*   1 quantity buttercream (see page 98)
*   Icing sugar for rolling out
*   700 g (1 lb 9 oz) yellow sugarpaste
*   100 g (3½ oz) flesh-coloured sugarpaste
*   50 g (2 oz) light brown sugarpaste
*   50 g (2 oz) darker brown sugarpaste
*   35 g (1¼ oz) pale blue sugarpaste
*   15 g (½ oz) white sugarpaste
*   Black food colour
*   20 small sweets

■ UTENSILS

*   Greaseproof paper
*   Pencil
*   Eraser
*   Sheet of clear perspex (about 20 cm x 13 cm/ 8 in x 5 in) (optional)
*   Pin or scriber (optional)
*   Piping bags (see page 102 for details)
*   Scissors
*   Number 2 or 3 piping nozzles
*   Clean damp cloth
*   Carving knife
*   25 cm (10 in) round cake board
*   Rolling pin
*   Cake smoother (optional)
*   Small sharp knife
*   Water
*   Medium and fine paintbrushes
*   Cocktail stick
*   150 cm (60 in) white ribbon

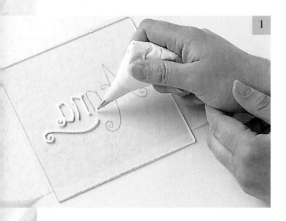

1   If you feel confident enough to pipe the baby's name directly on to the top of the cake without following a guide, go straight to step 2. If you're not, then one of these two solutions might help.

(a) Do this after you have covered the cake with sugarpaste. Write the baby's name on a piece of greaseproof paper. Place the paper, right way up, on the top of the cake and using either a cocktail stick, dressmaking pin or scriber (this is a sugarcraft tool especially designed for the job), trace over the lettering. Lift off the greaseproof paper and a scratched impression of the name should be left behind on the sugarpaste.

   Place about 15 ml (1 tbsp) royal icing into a piping bag fitted with a number 2 piping nozzle and secure the end. Pipe over the lettering.

   This method works best on a sugarpasted cake that has been allowed to harden overnight, otherwise it is very easy to dent the cake accidentally when leaning on it.

(b) Prepare this before you cover the cake with sugarpaste.

   Write the baby's name on greaseproof paper. Turn the greaseproof over so that the writing is still visible but now reads back to front. Place a small piece of perspex over the greaseproof. Pipe over the name with royal icing on to the perspex (*fig 1*).

   Put to one side, leave to dry and go on to step 2.

2   Level the top of the cake. Turn it upside down and place on the cake board. Slice and fill the centre with buttercream. Reassemble the cake and buttercream the sides and top.

   Dust the worksurface with a little icing sugar and knead and roll out 500 g (1 lb 2 oz) of yellow sugarpaste. Place this over the cake and carefully smooth it into position. Run over the surface with a cake smoother, if you have one, to iron out any bumps. Alternatively, use the flat of your hand. Trim away any excess sugarpaste from the base.

   Lightly moisten the exposed cake board with a little water. Roll out 200 g (7 oz) of yellow sugarpaste and cut out a strip approximately 61 cm (24 in) long and 3 cm (1¼ in) wide. Carefully roll up the sugarpaste strip, then unwind it to cover the cake board (see page 100). If you find this too time-consuming, you can leave the base uncovered.

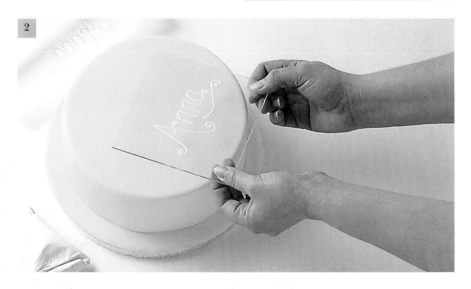

board. Starting from the back of the cake, hold the piping bag at a slight angle. Squeeze out a little icing, then release the pressure and pull slightly. Keep the tip of the nozzle in the icing all the time. Squeeze out a little more icing, release the pressure and pull (*fig 3*). Repeat all the way round the base of the cake.

You may wish to practise this technique on your worksurface first if you are not too confident of your piping skills. Alternatively, pipe a simple line of dots or stick sweets on the cake instead.

5 All the babies, dressed or undressed, are composed of the same six basic shapes (*fig 4*). To make the baby's body, roll 20 g (¾ oz) of flesh-coloured sugarpaste into a conical shape. Make the head by rolling 5 g (⅛ oz) of flesh-coloured sugarpaste into a small ball. Stick in place with a little water (*fig 5*).

Make the babies' legs by rolling approximately 10 g (¼ oz) of flesh-coloured sugarpaste into a sausage. Cut

3 If using the second method of writing, gently touch the royal icing on the perspex to check that it has dried. If it still feels soft, then place a bit of cling film over the top of the cake to stop the sugarpaste surface from hardening too much before the royal icing is ready. (The sugarpaste has to be soft enough to take an impression.) When the piping feels hard to the touch, turn the perspex over and press the lettering into the top of the cake (*fig 2*). Carefully pull it away. The baby's name should now be visible as an impression. Pipe over the name with white royal icing, using a number 2 nozzle.

4 When the name is on the top of the cake, pipe a 'snail trail' around the base of the cake to hide the join between cake and

TIP

To avoid damaging the sugarpasted cake, you may find it easier to make the models of the babies away from the cake and then stick them in position once they are finished.

this in two, then gently bend the end of each one to form a foot. Stick these in whatever position you wish.

For the arms, take about 5 g (⅛ oz) of sugarpaste and roll into a sausage. Cut in two and flatten one end of each half to make a hand. Stick these against the body. Thinly roll out a little white sugarpaste and cut out a tiny triangle. Stick this on as a nappy.

Paint the facial details with black food colour and a fine paintbrush, and stick two tiny dots of icing either side of the head for the ears and one in the middle of the face for a nose. To make a frilly mop hat, simply cut out a thin disc of white sugarpaste and roll a cocktail stick around the edge to frill it *(fig 6)*. Stick onto the back of the head and roll a tiny bit of yellow sugarpaste into a curl and stick onto the forehead.

6 Make as many or as few babies as you want (or you have time for), altering the positions of the hands and feet and giving each one an individual expression and different hair colour.

Use the same shapes for the baby in the romper suit, but use coloured sugarpaste for the arms, legs and body to look like the clothing.

7 To complete the cake, stick small sweets around the top and the board and tie a bow around the sides as the perfect finishing touch.

D e c o r a t i n g   v a r i a t i o n

As you can see, this cake works just as well in a different colour. If you prefer something paler, leave the base of the cake white and colour the piping instead. If you find it difficult to tie a bow, leave it off and add a couple more babies and sweets to fill the space instead.

Twitcher

There's a type of person who at the mere rumour of a lesser-spotted swamp gurgler near Congleton will miss appointments, cross continents and sit for hours in freezing conditions just to catch the merest sight. Weird, but it makes for a good cake!

INGREDIENTS

- 1 pudding basin cake (see page 94)
- 1 quantity buttercream (see page 98)
- Icing sugar for rolling out
- 260 g (9 oz) black sugarpaste
- 20 g (¾ oz) pale blue sugarpaste
- 10 g (¼ oz) flesh-coloured sugarpaste
- 50 g (2 oz) brown sugarpaste
- 10 g (¼ oz) white sugarpaste
- Black food colour
- 150 g (5 oz) dark green sugarpaste
- 150 g (5 oz) mid-green sugarpaste
- 150 g (5 oz) pale green sugarpaste
- Brown food colour
- 10 g (¼ oz) pale brown sugarpaste
- 10 g (¼ oz) very dark brown sugarpaste
- 20 g (¾ oz) yellow sugarpaste
- 30 g (1 oz) golden brown sugarpaste
- 30 g (1 oz) green-coloured desiccated coconut (see page 98)
- 30 g (1 oz) brown-coloured desiccated coconut

UTENSILS

- Carving knife
- 25 cm (10 in) round cake board
- Palette knife
- Rolling pin
- Water
- Medium and fine paintbrushes
- Small sharp knife
- Piping nozzle

1 Turn the cake upside down so that the widest part sits on the board. If it wobbles, cut a slice from the base so that it sits securely. Split it in half and fill the centre with buttercream and reassemble. Position the cake to the left of the board and then spread a layer of buttercream over the sides and top.

2 Dust the worksurface with icing sugar. Knead 250 g (9 oz) of black sugarpaste until it is pliable. Roll it out and place over the cake. Smooth it into position, and trim and neaten the base.

3 To make the twitcher, begin with his binoculars. Roll 5 g (⅛ oz) of black sugarpaste into a small sausage. Cut this in half and stick the two halves side by side, pointing outwards, on the front of the cake. If they start to droop at all, stick a little ledge of black sugarpaste underneath them to provide extra support.

Next, roll 20 g (¾ oz) of pale blue sugarpaste into a sausage. Cut this in half and bend each half slightly into a curved boomerang shape. Stick these pieces onto the cake with the flat, cut ends up against the binoculars.

4 To make the twitcher's head, roll a 5 g (⅛ oz) lump of flesh-coloured sugarpaste into a semi-circular shape. Stick this just above the binoculars.

Next, make two tiny flattened ovals of flesh-coloured sugarpaste for his hands

and stick these on top of the binoculars. Thinly roll out a little brown sugarpaste. Cut out and fringe a tiny rectangle. Stick this on top of his head (*fig 2*).

To make his ears, stick two tiny balls of flesh-coloured sugarpaste either side of his head and push the end of a paintbrush into each ear to add detail.

Thinly roll out a little white sugarpaste and cut out two tiny discs (a piping nozzle is useful for doing this). Stick the white circles to the ends of the binoculars and paint a small picture of a bird with black food colour (you can miss this stage out if you wish).

5 Roll out a small piece of each of the green sugarpastes and cut out some basic leaf

Cut out a diamond shape for his beak. Bend it in half and stick onto the face. Stick two tiny flattened balls of white sugarpaste onto his face for his eyes and paint in pupils and eyebrows with black food colour.

Roll out and cut two longish triangles for his wings and stick these either side of his body in an outraged, hands-on-hips position. Carefully place the bird on top of the cake.

9 Moisten the cake board with a little water and carefully spoon the coloured coconut around the base of the cake to look like grass and earth.

TIP
If the person you are making this cake for 'twitches' for something else, substitute flowers or butterflies or a train for the bird.

shapes. Press a simple vein pattern into each one using the back of a knife. Starting from the base, stick the leaves around the sides of the cake, alternating the different shades and allowing them to overlap until the entire cake has been covered *(fig 3)*.

6 To make the tree stump, mould 40 g (1 ¾ oz) of brown sugarpaste into a rounded stump shape with a flat base and top *(fig 1)*. Holding the back of a knife vertically, press irregular lines around the sides of the stump. Paint a wash of watered-down brown food colour around the stump to pick out the bark.

Cut out a thin disc of pale brown sugarpaste and stick on top of the stump. Paint a few age rings on the top with brown food colour.

Roll some little bits of leftover green sugarpaste into thin strings and stick these up against the sides of the stump. Place it in position on the board and secure with a little water.

7 To make the smaller bird, roll about 5 g (⅛ oz) of very dark brown sugarpaste into a tapering sausage shape *(fig 1)*. Bend the head end up slightly and flatten and pull the tail into a point.

Add two tiny flattened balls of white sugarpaste for his eyes and a tiny triangle of yellow for a beak. Stick two tiny dark brown triangles either side of the body for wings. Paint the pupils on the eyes with black food colour.

8 For the large bird, use 30 g (1 oz) of golden brown sugarpaste. Mould this into a rounded cone. Bend the smaller end over to make a head *(fig 1)*.

Roll out a little yellow sugarpaste and cut out a rectangle for the tail. Cut a triangle out of one end and stick it against the back of the bird.

Bride and Groom

A special feature of this cake is that as the models are on a thin cake board, they can be lifted off and kept as mementoes. If you prefer a rich fruit cake instead of sponge, cover with a layer of marzipan first.

■ INGREDIENTS

- 20 cm (8 in) round sponge cake
- 1 quantity buttercream (see page 98)
- Icing sugar for rolling out
- 800 g (1 lb 12 oz) cream-coloured sugarpaste
- 90 g (3 oz) grey sugarpaste
- 2 strands raw dried spaghetti
- 30 g (1 oz) flesh-coloured sugarpaste
- 150 g (5 oz) white sugarpaste
- 10 g (¼ oz) pink sugarpaste
- 5 g (⅛ oz) brown sugarpaste
- Black and gooseberry green food colour pastes
- 30 g (1 oz) black sugarpaste
- 5 g (⅛ oz) yellow sugarpaste
- 90 g (3 oz) green sugarpaste
- ½ quantity royal icing (see page 99)

■ UTENSILS

- Carving knife
- 25 cm (10 in) round cake board
- Rolling pin
- Cake smoother (optional)
- Small sharp knife
- 15 cm (6 in) round thin cake board
- Water
- Fine and medium paintbrushes
- Templates for shirt, jacket and veil (see page 109)
- 2 piping bags (see page 102)
- 150 cm (60 in) ivory ribbon

1 Level the top of the cake, spread with buttercream and cover both the cake and board with 700 g (1 lb 9 oz) of cream-coloured sugarpaste as described in step 2 of the christening cake on page 50. Place the cake to one side.

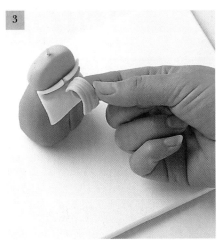

2 Cover the thin 15 cm (6 in) round cake board with 60 g (2 oz) of cream-coloured sugarpaste as described on page 100. Trim and neaten the edges. Place this to one side too.

3 On a spare board or worksurface, make the groom. Roll 80 g (2¾ oz) of grey sugarpaste into a chunky conical shape about 7 cm (2¼ in) tall. Check that the base is flat so that it stands upright. To add extra internal support, insert a strand of dried spaghetti into the body, leaving about 4 cm (1½ in) protruding out of the top (*fig 1*).

4 Roll 15 g (½ oz) of flesh-coloured sugarpaste into an oval shape (*fig 2*). Stick onto the body (use a little water as well), leaving about 1 cm (⅜ in) of spaghetti still protruding.

   Make his shirt by rolling out about 10 g (¼ oz) of white sugarpaste and cutting out a rectangle, using the template if necessary. Make a little cut in the centre of the top edge. Stick this to the front of the

body, allowing the collar to just overlap the face. Bend the collar forwards slightly.

5 To make the cravat, roll a tiny piece of pink sugarpaste into a thin string. Stick this just under the collar. Roll out a little more pink and cut into a thin, tapering rectangular shape. Press lines down the length of the strip using the back of a knife. Stick this in place on the front of the shirt (*fig 3*).

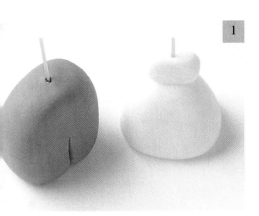

6 Roll out a tiny strip of brown sugarpaste. Cut out a thinnish rectangle and press lines down its length. Moisten the top of the head and lay this across for his hair.

Stick three tiny balls of flesh-coloured sugarpaste on the head for his ears and nose and push the end of a paintbrush into each ear to add detail. Paint his features with black food colour.

   To make the hat, roll out 10 g (¼ oz) of grey sugarpaste. Cut out a circle about 3.5 cm (1½ in) in diameter and stick onto the head. Re-knead the rest of the grey and mould into a rounded shape with a flat base and top. Stick onto the head and bend up the sides of the brim.

7 To make the jacket, roll out 20 g (¾ oz) of the black sugarpaste. Cut out a jacket shape, using the template if necessary. Make a cut for the tails and wrap and stick the jacket around the groom's body (any gaps in the tummy area will be hidden by his arm at a later stage). Place the groom to one side.

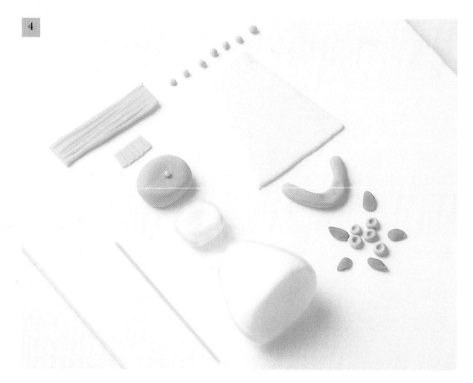

some on the bride's front to make a bouquet. Intersperse the flowers with tiny bits of green sugarpaste. Push little hollows in each flower with the end of a paintbrush.

11 Stick the bride and groom next to each other on the covered board and then make the groom's arms. Roll 10 g (¼ oz) of black sugarpaste into a sausage. Cut it in two. Bend one half into a right-angle and stick on the front of the groom. Position and stick the other one so that it looks as though the groom has his arm around the bride (*fig 6*).

Add two flattened balls of flesh-coloured sugarpaste for the hands.

8 Make the bride's skirt by rolling 50 g (2 oz) of white sugarpaste into a pointed conical shape. Stick a 5 g (⅛ oz) oval of white sugarpaste on top (*fig 1*). Insert a strand of dried spaghetti as you did for the groom. Roll 5 g (⅛ oz) of flesh-coloured sugarpaste into a ball for her head (*fig 4*) and stick it to the body. Paint her features with black food colour and a fine brush and stick a tiny piece of flesh-coloured sugarpaste on the front of her face for a nose. Roll a little flesh-coloured icing into a thin sausage for her arms. Stick this onto the front of the body in a 'U' shape.

9 To make the hair, roll a little yellow sugarpaste into a thin strip about 6 cm

(2½ in) long. Press lines into it with a knife, then lay and stick it over the bride's head (*fig 5*). Tweak the ends up into a curl. Make a tiny yellow rectangle for a fringe. Press lines into this also and stick on her forehead.

10 To make her veil, roll out 15 g (½ oz) of white sugarpaste. Cut out a veil, using the template if necessary. Moisten the bride's head and back and stick it in place.

Stick a line of tiny pink sugarpaste balls along the edge of the veil and one on the groom's jacket as a buttonhole. Also stick

12 To make a rose, use about 10 g (¼ oz) of white or cream sugarpaste. Roll the icing into a thin strip. Paint a line of water down one side and roll up the icing (*fig 7*). Tweak the petals into position and slice a little away from the base so the rose can stand up. Make a total of at least eight roses in this way.

13 To make a bud, roll about 5 g (⅛ oz) of sugarpaste into a sausage with two pointed ends. Press a line down the top and bend it into an 'S' shape.

14 For the leaves, roll out a little of the green sugarpaste and cut out a few very basic leaf shapes. Press a simple vein pattern into each one with the back of a knife and stick the roses, leaves and buds around the bride and groom. Add little swirls of green food colour and dots of royal icing, too, if you like.

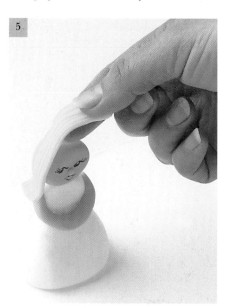

Little monster

Not only is this a quick cake to make but it's a useful one because you can use odd bits of coloured sugarpaste to cover the monster. This cake was designed as a child's cake, but I know quite a few grown-up monsters it would suit too!

■ INGREDIENTS

- 1 pudding bowl cake (see page 94)
- 1 quantity buttercream (see page 98)
- Icing sugar for rolling out
- 400 g (14 oz) multi-coloured mixture of various coloured sugarpastes (eg green, white, orange, blue, yellow and red)
- 110 g (4 oz) white sugarpaste
- 30 g (1 oz) black sugarpaste
- Red food colour
- Liquorice or strawberry bootlace
- 100 g (3½ oz) coloured sugar or 'Hundreds and Thousands'

■ UTENSILS

- Carving knife
- 25 cm (10 in) round cake board
- Rolling pin
- Small sharp knife
- Piping nozzle
- Water
- Medium and fine paintbrushes
- Cocktail stick

1 Place the cake upside down with the widest part forming the base and cut irregular lumps and bumps out of the cake (*fig 1*). Slice and fill the middle of the cake with a layer of buttercream. Reassemble the cake and place it on the board. 'Glue' the cut-out lumps around the sides and top of the cake with buttercream. Spread a layer of buttercream over the top and sides.

2 Roll out 300 g (10½ oz) of the multi-coloured sugarpaste (*fig 2*) and use this to cover the cake. Smooth it into position over the cake, taking care to press out any air trapped in the hollows. Trim, neaten and cut the excess from the base. Add the effect of scales by pressing something circular, such as a cutter or a piping nozzle held at an angle, into the icing.

3 To make his eyes, take two 25 g (¾ oz) lumps of white sugarpaste. Roll them both into ball shapes then flatten slightly. Stick them to the front of his face.

Roll out 10 g (¼ oz) of black sugarpaste and cut out two flat discs (your piping nozzle will come in useful again to do this). Stick the discs onto the eyes. Flatten two tiny balls of white sugarpaste and stick these onto the black for highlights. Finish off each eye by painting a few ghoulish blood vessels with red food colour and a fine paintbrush (*fig 3*).

4 To make his whiskers, cut liquorice or strawberry bootlace into twelve shortish sections of between 5 cm and 9 cm (2 in and 3½ in). Poke three holes above and below each eye using a cocktail stick and insert a length of bootlace into each one.

5 For his ears, take 100 g (4 oz) of the multi-coloured sugarpaste. Divide it in two and mould each half into a slightly misshapen triangular shape. Stick the ears to the sides of the head.

6 Roll 10 g (¼ oz) of the multi-coloured sugarpaste into a round ball and stick onto the front of the face to make the monster's nose.

7 To make the mouth, thinly roll out 20 g (¾ oz) of black sugarpaste and cut out a wonky smiling shape. Stick this onto the face. Roll out 10 g (¼ oz) of white sugarpaste and cut out three rectangles of slightly different sizes. Stick these onto the mouth to give the monster a gap-toothed smile.

8 To make the hands, roll 20 g (¾ oz) of white sugarpaste into a ball then flatten it slightly. Cut the resulting disc in half. Make three partial cuts into each semi-circle and then splay the cuts out to make the fingers. Stick one hand on either side of the body.

9 To make the feet, take 20 g (¾ oz) of white sugarpaste. Roll it into a flattish circle the same as for the hands and cut it in half. Stick the two semi-circles against the monster's body. Press some lines into each foot using the back of a knife.

10 Lightly moisten the exposed cake board with a little water and sprinkle with coloured sugar or 'hundreds and thousands'.

Sports car

This will suit anyone with a passion for fast cars and will disappear off the tea table speedily too! It's also very versatile – see how the basic shape can be adapted into an aeroplane (page 65). The rocks double up as candle holders.

(page 65)

- Cake baked in loaf tin (see page 94 for details)
- 1 quantity buttercream (see page 98)
- Icing sugar for rolling out
- 250 g (9 oz) green sugarpaste
- 130 g (4½ oz) flesh-coloured sugarpaste
- 110 g (3¾ oz) brown sugarpaste
- 120 g (4 oz) white sugarpaste
- 150 g (5 oz) black sugarpaste
- 40 g (1½ oz) grey sugarpaste
- 40 g (1½ oz) cream sugarpaste
- Black and green food colour pastes
- 60 g (2 oz) desiccated coconut

■ **UTENSILS**

- Carving knife
- Palette knife
- 25 cm (10 in) square cake board
- Rolling pin
- Small sharp knife
- Water and paintbrush
- Circle cutters or similar
- 2 small bowls

1 Stand the cake up with the thinnest part at the bottom. Cut two triangular pieces away from the sides to form the bonnet. Cut a slope into the top of the bonnet too. Level the remaining top section of the cake where the driver will eventually sit and round all the top edges slightly to form the basic shape *(fig 1)*.

Slice and fill the middle of the cake with buttercream. Reassemble and place it diagonally on the cake board. Spread a thin layer of buttercream over the top and sides of the cake.

2 Dust the worksurface with icing sugar and knead and roll out the green sugarpaste. Carefully lift this over the cake and gently smooth into position. Trim and neaten the base.

3 To make the driver, first roll 100 g (3½ oz) of flesh-coloured sugarpaste into a flattish oval shape *(fig 2)*. Stick this with a little water towards the back of the car.

Roll 70 g (2½ oz) of brown sugarpaste into a ball then flatten the base to make a semi-circular shape for the driver's helmet. Stick this on top of his head. Roll out about another 10 g (¼ oz) of brown sugarpaste and cut out a thin, flat semi-circle. Stick this to the front of the helmet to form the brim *(fig 3)*.

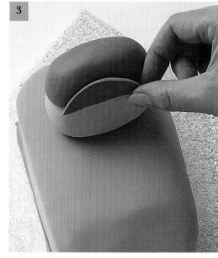

4 For the eyes, roll out 10 g (¼ oz) of white sugarpaste to a thickness of 5 mm (¼ in) and cut out two discs about 2 cm (¾ in) in diameter. If you don't have a circle cutter this size and can't find a lid or anything else to use as a cutter, simply divide the icing into two, roll each half into a ball, then squash each ball down to the right size. Finish off the eyes by sticking two tiny flattened balls of black sugarpaste onto the

arm at the elbow and bend each one into a right-angle. Stick an arm on each side of the body.

Finish off the arms by sticking on a pair of hands made from small flattened circles of flesh-coloured sugarpaste. Arrange the hands so that they hold onto the steering wheel.

8 To make the ear flaps for the helmet, roll out approximately 15 g (½ oz) of brown sugarpaste. Cut out two small oval shapes. If you find cutting out an oval using the tip of your knife too fiddly, cut out a circle instead using a small lid or circle cutter, then gently pull it into shape. Another method is to cut out a rectangle, slice off the corners and gently smooth the edges into an oval.

When you have made your oval shapes, stick one either side of the helmet for the flaps (*fig 6*). Next, cut two tiny strips for his helmet straps and stick one on either flap.

white for his pupils and a small sausage of black over the top for his eyebrows.

5 To make the scarf, roll out the cream sugarpaste. Cut into a strip about 28 cm x 2.5 cm (11 in x 1 in). Cut a fringe into both ends and paint a line of water around the driver's neck. Lay the scarf into position (*fig 4*). Tweak the ends up slightly into a jaunty, 'blowing in the wind' angle.

6 Roll a pea-sized ball of flesh-coloured sugarpaste and stick onto the driver's face

for his nose. Knead and shape about 10 g (¼ oz) of grey sugarpaste into a thickish semi-circle for the steering wheel. Stick this in front of the driver.

Roll 20 g (¾ oz) of black sugarpaste into a sausage about 25 cm (10 in) long. Starting from the back, lay and stick this on top of the car, around the driver (*fig 5*).

7 To make the driver's arms, roll about 15 g (½ oz) of brown sugarpaste into a sausage about 10 cm (4 in) long. Cut it in half. Make two partial cuts in the centre of each

TIP

To personalize your car, write the recipient's name, age or a short message on the number plate using black food colour and a paintbrush.

9 To make the wheels, roll out about 125 g (4¼ oz) of black sugarpaste to a thickness of about 5 mm (¼ in). Cut out two discs about 6 cm (2¼ in) in diameter. Scrunch up the leftover icing. Re-roll it and cut out another two discs. Stick the wheels into position (*fig 7*).

Roll out about 10 g (¼ oz) of white sugarpaste and cut out four smaller and much thinner discs. If you haven't got anything suitable to cut out a circle with, simply divide the sugarpaste into four. Roll each quarter into a ball and flatten to the required size. These circles form the centres of the wheels. Stick them neatly into position.

10 For the bumpers, roll 30 g (1 oz) of grey sugarpaste out to a thickness of about 5 mm (¼ in). Cut out two strips. The first should measure about 8 cm (3 in) long by 2 cm (¾ in) wide. Stick this around the front of the car. The back bumper should measure about 15 cm x 2 cm (6 in x ¾ in). Stick this into place too.

11 To make the headlights, take another 10 g (¼ oz) of grey sugarpaste and roll this into an egg shape. Cut it in half and stick both halves to the front of the bonnet. Thinly roll out about 20 g (¾ oz) of white sugarpaste and cut out two small discs. Stick one disc onto the front of each headlight.

Also cut out two small rectangles for the number plates and stick them to the front and back of the car.

12 Place 20 g (¾ oz) of the desiccated coconut in one of the bowls and colour it green by mixing in a little green food colour paste. Colour the rest grey in another bowl with a little black food paste.

Decorating variation

To adapt the car into an aeroplane, the same basic body shape was covered with grey sugarpaste. The wings and tail were made out of grey-coloured gelatin icing (see page 99) and allowed to harden overnight. (Turn the components over after about 4-5 hours to allow the undersides to dry out as well.) They were attached to the body of the plane with royal icing and supported by balls of scrunched up clingfilm placed underneath the wings while drying in position. Add a propeller to the front of the plane. Decorate the nose of the plane and the wings with circles of coloured sugarpaste. The cake board was covered in pale blue sugarpaste and decorated with white cut-out clouds and birds painted in black food colour.

Lightly moisten the exposed cake board with a few drops of water. Carefully spoon the grey coconut immediately around the car then spoon the green over the edges. To make things easier and quicker, you could colour all the coconut just one shade if you prefer.

13 Finally, to make the rocks, partially knead about 80 g (2¾ oz) of white sugarpaste and about 20 g (¾ oz) of black together for a marbled effect. Pull off irregular sized lumps and stick these along the side of the road. These rocks can also be used as candle holders.

Chocolate box

A wonderful cake suitable for all sorts of occasions – birthdays, Valentine's day, Mother's day, anniversaries or any chocoholic type of day (and you don't need much of an excuse for those!).

■ INGREDIENTS

- 15 cm (6 in) round sponge cake
- ½ quantity buttercream (see page 98)
- Icing sugar for rolling out
- 100 g (3 oz) black sugarpaste
- 300 g (10 oz) pink sugarpaste
- 30 g (1 oz) bag white chocolate buttons
- 227 g (½ lb) box milk chocolates
- 200 g (7 oz) white sugarpaste

■ UTENSILS

- Carving knife
- 23 cm (9 in) round cake board
- Rolling pin
- 15 cm (6 in) round thin cake board
- Small sharp knife
- Ruler
- Heart-shaped cutter
- Drinking straw
- Water and paintbrush
- 70 cm (30 in) ribbon

1 Level the cake if necessary then turn it upside down and place onto the cake board. Slice and fill the centre with buttercream and spread a thin layer of buttercream around the top and sides.

2 Knead and roll out all the black sugarpaste on a work surface dusted with icing sugar. Using the thin 15 cm (6 in) cake board as a template, cut out a black disc and lay this on top of the cake. Clean your hands, rolling pin and worksurface to avoid getting black sooty smudges everywhere.

3 Measure the height of the cake. Sprinkle the worksurface with icing sugar and roll out 200 g (7 oz) of pink sugarpaste so that you can cut out a strip about 46 cm (18 in) long and about 1 cm (½ in) wider than the depth of your cake (this cake measured about 9 cm/3½ in). Roll the icing up like a bandage, making sure it is not too tight or you will have problems unwinding it. Dust with more icing sugar if it seems to be sticking and then unwind it around the side of the cake (*fig 1*).

If the icing won't stick, it probably means the previous buttercream covering around the sides has dried out so simply spread another thin layer to provide better adhesion. Neaten and trim away any excess from the base and the join.

4 Using a heart-shaped cutter and a drinking straw, press a pattern around the side of the box.

5 Carefully paint a light line of water around the inside edge of the black disc. Neatly press a line of white chocolate buttons vertically into the black icing, allowing them to rest against the pink sugarpaste (*fig 2*).

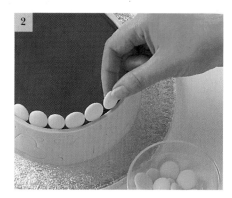

6 Arrange the chocolates in the top of the box, securing them in position with dabs of buttercream. Unfortunately, this arrangement uses up most of a 227 g (½ lb) box of milk chocolates, leaving only a couple left over for the cook. Stick one of these on top of the chocolates to support the lid and sample the leftovers – all for purely professional taste testing purposes, of course!

7 Moisten the top and sides of the thin cake board with a little water, roll out and cover with 100 g (3 oz) of pink sugarpaste. Trim and neaten the edges and press the heart cutter and drinking straw into the icing to echo the pattern around the sides. Place the lid to one side temporarily whilst you cover the base to avoid it from getting damaged.

8 Moisten the exposed cake board with a little water. Knead and roll 200 g (7 oz) white sugarpaste into a strip. Roll it up, then unwind it around the board allowing it to fall into folds like fabric as you go (see page 101). Press the icing down neatly at the edges of the board and trim away any excess.

9 Place a small dab of buttercream on top of the highest chocolate. Place the lid in position on top.

10 Make a bow out of the ribbon and attach this to the cake with a little more buttercream.

TIP

For a completely edible box (if you have time), you could make the lid out of pink-coloured gelatin icing as shown on page 99 and decorate this with an icing bow.

Gardener's delight

A novel cake for budding gardeners. It could be decorated with flowers instead if you prefer – see page 57 for effective but extremely fast roses. If you're not keen on marzipan, this cake looks just as effective made up in sugarpaste.

■ INGREDIENTS

- Flowerpot-shaped cake (see step 1)
- 1 quantity buttercream (see page 98)
- Icing sugar for rolling out
- 920 g (2 lb) white marzipan
- Paprika, red, green, dark brown, black, orange and yellow food colour pastes
- 60 g (2 oz) dark brown sugar

■ UTENSILS

- 23 cm (9 in) round cake board
- Carving knife
- Palette knife
- Rolling pin
- Tape measure
- Water and paintbrush
- Small sharp knife

1 The easiest way to make a cake of this shape is to bake the cake itself in a new 15 cm (6 in) terracotta plant pot. Simply wash the pot out, grease and line it with greaseproof paper. Use the same amounts given on page 94 for a 15 cm (6 in) square cake. Level the top of the cake and turn upside down so the widest part sits on the board. Slice and fill the centre with buttercream and spread extra buttercream around the top and sides.

2 Colour 550 g (1 lb 4 oz) marzipan terracotta using paprika food colour paste. If you can't obtain paprika colour, use a mixture of red, yellow and a hint of brown. Roll out 400 g (14 oz) on a worksurface dusted with icing sugar and cover the cake. Smooth over the top and sides and trim any excess from the base.

3 Re-knead the excess into the rest of the terracotta-coloured marzipan. Roll it out and cut out a strip about 46 cm x 4 cm (18 in x 1½ in). Paint a line of water around the base of the cake. Wind up the marzipan strip like a bandage. Then, starting from the back, unwind it around the base of the cake so it resembles the lip of a real flowerpot (*fig 1*). Neaten the join.

4 To make the tomatoes, colour 50 g (1¾ oz) marzipan red. Roll into two balls and make a dent in the top of each one with the end of a paintbrush. Roll out about 5 g (⅛ oz) green-coloured marzipan and cut out two rough star shapes. Stick one on the top of each tomato with a little water (*fig 2*).

5 For the potatoes, roll 120 g (4 oz) of white marzipan into two misshapen oval shapes. Leave them like this for the moment as they are easier to paint once in position.

6 For the carrots, colour 60 g (2 oz) of marzipan orange. Divide into three and roll into carrot shapes. Press a few lines across the top using the back of a knife. Roll out 5 g (⅛ oz) of green marzipan and cut out three irregular rectangles. Make cuts down almost the whole length of each shape and fringe. Stick one on each carrot.

7 For the peas, simply colour about 10 g (¼ oz) of marzipan a pale green colour and roll into small balls.

8 For the pepper, colour 80 g (2¾ oz) of marzipan yellow and roll into a conical shape. Press small grooves into the sides and top and finish with some green marzipan bent into a stalk.

9 Arrange the vegetables around the base of the flowerpot, securing them with a little water. Make sure the join on the lip of the flowerpot is hidden at the back. Moisten the exposed cake board with a little water and spoon the dark brown sugar around the board to look like soil.

10 Paint the potatoes with a wash of watered-down brown food colour. Finish with tiny dots of black food colour and also paint a black circle on the top of the cake to look like the hole in the top of the flowerpot.

11 Roll out 40 g (1½ oz) of green marzipan and cut out some leaves. Press a few veins in each one using the back of a knife and stick these around the flowerpot.

Cheeky rabbits

On this design the cake and board are covered all in one go. If you don't feel comfortable doing it this way, cover the cake first and then the board separately. Hide any tears under rocks and rabbits later.

■ INGREDIENTS

- 20 cm (8 in) round sponge cake
- 1 quantity buttercream (see page 98)
- Icing sugar for rolling out
- 600 g (1 lb 5 oz) mid-green sugarpaste
- 20 g (¾ oz) black sugarpaste
- 200 g (7 oz) grey sugarpaste
- 70 g (2½ oz) white sugarpaste
- 10 g (¼ oz) flesh-coloured sugarpaste
- 40 g (1¾ oz) pink sugarpaste
- 30 g (1 oz) orange sugarpaste
- 10 g (¼ oz) dark green sugarpaste

■ UTENSILS

- Carving knife
- 25 cm (10 in) round cake board
- Palette knife
- Water and paintbrush
- Rolling pin
- Small sharp knife
- Wooden spoon
- Five-petal flower cutter (optional)
- Piping nozzle

1 Carve the cake into an irregular shape by cutting out lumps and bumps *(fig 1)*. Place some of the cut-out pieces on top of the cake to increase its height and some around the edges. 'Glue' all the cut out pieces in place with dabs of buttercream, then slice and fill the middle of the cake with more buttercream. Spread a thin covering of buttercream over the outside of the cake as well.

2 Dust the worksurface with icing sugar and knead the mid-green sugarpaste until pliable. Lightly moisten the exposed cake board with a little water. Roll out the sugarpaste, then lift and place it over both the cake and the board. Starting from the middle of the cake and trying to expel any trapped air, smooth the icing into position. Trim and neaten the edges around the board.

3 To make the rabbit popping out of the burrow, first roll out about 10 g (¼ oz) of the black sugarpaste and cut out a flat disc about 5 cm (2 in) in diameter. Stick this on top of the cake with a little water.

Roll 5 g (⅛ oz) of grey sugarpaste into a sausage, cut this in two and flatten both halves to make the paws. Stick these onto the edge of the burrow.

To make the head, roll 50 g (2 oz) of grey sugarpaste into a cone. Flatten the cone slightly, making sure it can still stand upright. Make a cut from the tip of the cone to about one-third of the way down the centre of the head. Pull the two sections apart slightly to make his ears and add detail by pressing a paintbrush lightly into each one *(fig 2)*. Stick the head onto the paws.

4 Roll out about 10 g (¼ oz) of white sugarpaste. Cut out a tiny rectangle for rabbits teeth and two small round discs for

Make arms for the sitting up rabbit by rolling 5 g (⅛ oz) of grey sugarpaste into a thin sausage. Cut it in half and stick the two paws as though they are holding the carrot. Roll out the dark green sugarpaste and cut into small, thin strips. Fringe each strip and stick one on the end of each carrot.

8 To make the rocks, partially knead together 20 g (¾ oz) of grey sugarpaste and 40 g (1 ¾ oz) of white. Pull off small lumps and mould into irregular rock-like shapes. Dot these around the cake.

9 For the flowers, roll out a little pink sugarpaste. If using the flower cutter, cut out a flower shape or if using a piping nozzle, cut out five pink circles and arrange them in a circle. Place the flower on the cake and top with a small central circle of white sugarpaste. Make about six flowers in this way and position them around the cake.

his eyes (*fig 2*) – a small piping nozzle is useful for cutting out these. Make a small cut in the middle of the rectangle and stick both the teeth and the eyes in position. Make two tiny balls of black sugarpaste and flatten them. Stick these onto the eyes for his pupils.

Roll out 5 g (⅛ oz) of flesh-coloured sugarpaste and cut out two slightly larger circles for his muzzle. Stick these over the teeth. Finish off the rabbit's face with a tiny, flattened ball of pink sugarpaste for a nose.

5 To make the seated rabbit, roll 50 g (2 oz) of grey sugarpaste into a flattish circle for the body. Stick this against the cake. Roll out about 5 g (⅛ oz) of white sugarpaste and cut out a small circle. Stick this to his tummy.

Make another head as before and stick this onto the body. If the head starts to fall backwards, support it from behind with a bit of grey sugarpaste, and tell anyone who spots it that it's a rock and is supposed to be there!

6 For his feet, roll two 10 g (¼ oz) lumps of grey sugarpaste into oval shapes then flatten them both slightly. Stick them onto the front of the body and make three dents into the end of each one using the end of a wooden spoon or paintbrush. Cut out and stick a small white disc onto each foot too.

7 To make the carrots, divide the orange sugarpaste into six and roll each bit into a carrot shape. Using the back of a knife, press a few lines into the top of each one (*fig 3*). Take a 'bite' out of one using a piping nozzle. Stick the bitten carrot onto the front of the rabbit and the rest around the board.

TIP

This cake also introduces a five-petal flower cutter that, amongst other things, can be used to produce these marvellous bold cartoon-type flowers. These cutters are available from specialist cake shops but if you don't wish to buy one, an alternative method using a piping nozzle is also shown.

If you want to cut down on the modelling, have both bunnies popping out of burrows.

Horse and rider

If making this cake for someone who owns a horse, try to copy the markings and hair colour of the characters involved. To make a male rider, simply shorten the hair. You can substitute buttercream for the royal icing if you wish.

1 Level the top of the cake, if necessary, turn upside down and place in the middle of the cake board. Slice and fill the centre of the cake with a layer of buttercream. Reassemble the cake and then spread a thin covering of buttercream around the sides and top.

2 Dust the worksurface with icing sugar and knead and roll out 300 g (10½ oz) of white sugarpaste. Carefully lift the icing and place it over the cake. Smooth it into position and trim and neaten the base. Place the cake to one side while you make the horse.

3 Begin with the body. Roll 50 g (2 oz) of golden brown sugarpaste into a tapering cone shape. Lie this on its side (*fig 1*). Make the head out of 20 g (¾ oz) of golden brown sugarpaste. Pull off two tiny bits and keep for the ears. Roll the rest into an oval shape. Lightly squeeze the centre to make one rounded end bigger than the other. This bigger end will form the horse's nose. Stick the head onto the body and make dents for nostrils using the end of a paintbrush.

4 Make a saddle out of 5 g (⅛ oz) of dark brown sugarpaste. First cut out and stick a tiny, thin strip across the horse's back. Roll the rest of the dark brown into an oval shape, then flatten it slightly. Stick this onto the girth.

5 To make the forelegs, roll 10 g (¼ oz) of the golden-brown icing into a sausage. Cut this in two and bend each leg in half. Stick these against the body.
   To make the hind legs, roll 20 g (½ oz) of golden brown sugarpaste into a sausage approximately 10 cm (4 in) long. Again, divide the sausage in two and bend both halves. As you stick them against the sides of the horse, slightly flatten the top section of the leg.

Make two tiny triangular ears out of the leftover icing and stick these onto the head. Press a paintbrush into each ear to add some detail. Carefully position the horse on top of the cake and secure in place with a little water.

6 To make the rider's head, take 10 g (¼ oz) of flesh-coloured sugarpaste. Pull off a tiny piece for a nose and roll the rest into a ball. Stick the nose into position and paint eyes and a disgruntled mouth using black food colour.

7 Partially mix a little blue food colour into 30 ml (2 tbsp) of royal icing and smear this on the top of the cake in a sort of kidney

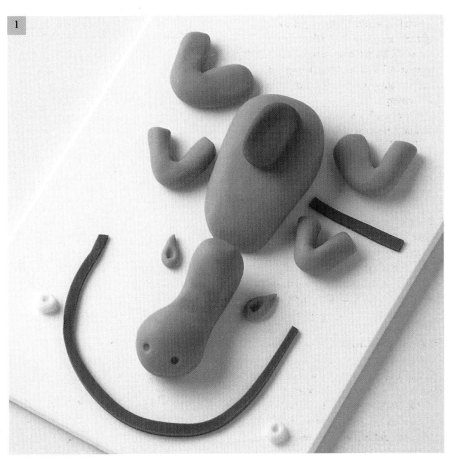

1

shape. Place the rider's head in the water. Make her hair by rolling out a little dark brown sugarpaste and cutting it into a rectangle. Press lines down the length of the rectangle with the back of a knife. Moisten the top of the rider's head and lay the hair in position (*fig 2*).

Make a riding hat by rolling 5 g (⅛ oz) of black sugarpaste into a round lump, then flatten the base so that it will sit on her head. Pinch a peak into the front of the hat and stick in position.

8   Partially knead 20 g (¾ oz) of black sugarpaste into 100 g (3½ oz) of white. Pull off little lumps and stick around the edge of the pond and the base of the cake to look like rocks.

Paint some watered-down green food colour around the horse and pond (gooseberry food colour paste is the ideal shade for this).

9   Mix a tiny bit of yellow food colour into 15 ml (1 tbsp) of royal icing to turn it

cream. Place the icing in a piping bag and snip about 2 mm (⅛ in) off the end. Pipe the horse's mane and tail using a squiggly motion (*fig 3*).

10 Colour 30 ml (2 tbsp) of royal icing light green and place into a piping bag. Do the same with some darker green royal icing. Snip the ends off both piping bags and pipe wiggly lines of greenery up the sides of the cake.

11 Finally, to finish off the horse, roll out a little dark brown sugarpaste. Cut out a long, thin strip for the horse's reins and lay this over the nose and around the back of the horse. Stick a tiny ball of white sugarpaste either side of the mouth and push a small hole in each one using the end of a paintbrush.

TIP
If you have problems making piping bags, your local cake decorating equipment shop should stock ready-made ones. Alternatively, you can buy tubes of 'writing' icing which could also be used to make the mane and tail.

Golfing star

A fun way of incorporating a person's favourite sport into a design is to base the cake itself on a piece of equipment such as a golf bag or a tennis racquet, then make a small model of the recipient dressed in the appropriate outfit.

INGREDIENTS

- Icing sugar for rolling out
- 300 g (10½ oz) green sugarpaste
- 15 cm (6 in) square cake
- 1 quantity buttercream (see page 98)
- 360 g (12½ oz) white sugarpaste
- 50 g (2 oz) grey sugarpaste
- 70 g (2¼ oz) dark brown sugarpaste
- 90 g (3¼ oz) red sugarpaste
- 50 g (2 oz) light brown sugarpaste
- 40 g (1¾ oz) blue sugarpaste
- 30 g (1 oz) flesh-coloured sugarpaste
- 10 g (¼ oz) black sugarpaste

UTENSILS

- 30 cm (12 in) round cake board
- Water
- Paintbrush
- Rolling pin
- Small sharp knife
- Cake smoother (optional)
- Carving knife
- Fish slice (optional)
- Palette knife
- Piping nozzle

1 Moisten the cake board with a little water. Sprinkle some icing sugar onto the worksurface and knead the green sugarpaste until it becomes pliable. Begin to roll it out into a thick, flattish disc, then lift and place the sugarpaste on the cake board. Continue to roll the icing up to and over the edges of the board. Trim and neaten the edges.

 If you possess one, run a cake smoother over the surface of the board to iron out any lumps and bumps. Alternatively, use the flat of your hand and strategically position the cake, figure and golf clubs over the worst bits later! Place the covered board to one side.

2 Cut the cake into shape by slicing about 5 cm (2 in) off one side. Place this against one of the now shorter sides to increase the length of the bag. Now cut the cake into a more recognisable bag shape by making two diagonal cuts at the top of the bag to give it a tapering neck and also cut a slope into the neck of the bag (*fig 1*). Round all the corners slightly.

3 Slice and fill the middle of the cake with a layer of buttercream, then spread a thin covering of buttercream over the top and sides. Wipe away any crumbs from the worksurface and dust with icing sugar.

Knead and roll out 300 g (10½ oz) of white sugarpaste. Lift and place over the cake. Smooth the icing into position and trim away any excess from the base. Carefully lift the cake and place on the covered cake board. (You may find using a fish slice to lift the cake helps to prevent fingerprints on the icing.)

4 Roll and shape about 20 g (¾ oz) of grey sugarpaste into a sort of tennis racquet shape. Bend the large, rounded end over to one side to make a golf club and stick onto the board at the neck of the bag.

 To make the wooden club, roll 40 g (1½ oz) of brown sugarpaste into a more rounded club shape. Stick a small flat oval of grey sugarpaste onto the top of the club and stick into position. Press a few lines into the top of the first club using the back of a knife (*fig 2*).

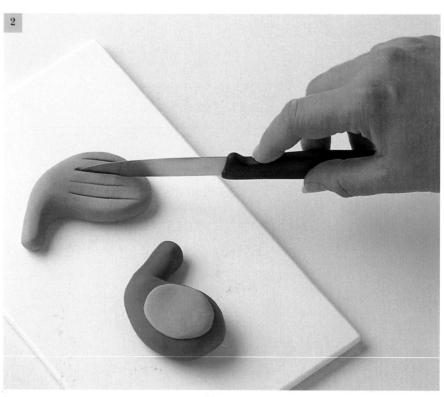

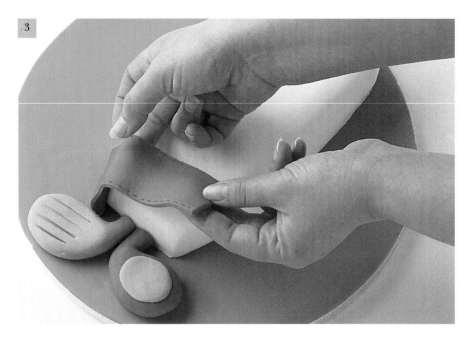

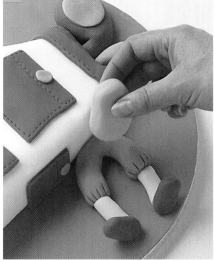

5 Roll out 20 g (¾ oz) of red sugarpaste and cut out a strip about 2.5 cm x 13 cm (1 in x 5 in). Make a series of small cuts along the two longer sides using just the tip of your knife to look like stitching. Lightly moisten the back of the strip with a little water and lay this over the base of the golf clubs and the neck of the bag (fig 3).

6 Roll out a further 70 g (2½ oz) of red sugarpaste and cut out four rectangles of varying sizes. Stick two on the front of the bag and two on the sides. Press the back of a knife across each one to leave a line looking like a flap. Using the tip of your

knife again, 'stitch' around each pocket (fig 4). Finish off each pocket with a button made from a small flattened ball of grey sugarpaste.

7 To make the golfer himself, begin with his legs. Roll about 40 g (1½ oz) of light brown sugarpaste into a sausage about 13 cm (5 in) long. Slightly bend the sausage into a 'U' shape and press a few lines into both ends to look like folds in the fabric. Stick this on the board towards the neck of the bag. Roll 20 g (¾ oz) of yellow sugarpaste into a sausage and cut in half. Stick one onto the end of each leg for his socks. Roll two 10 g (¼ oz) lumps of dark brown sugarpaste into two oval

shapes for his feet and stick one on the end of each sock.

Make a body by rolling about 40 g (1¾ oz) of blue sugarpaste into a cone and stick this on top of the legs (fig 5).

8 To make the arms, roll 20 g (¾ oz) of blue sugarpaste into a sausage and cut in half. Stick one arm either side of the body, allowing them to rest on the legs and the side of the golf bag itself. Slightly flatten a small ball of blue sugarpaste to make a thickish disc for the golfer's polo neck (fig 6). Stick this on top of the body.

9 Make a head by rolling 10 g (¼ oz) of flesh-coloured sugarpaste into a ball. Stick this onto the neck. Give him a smiling mouth by pressing a piping nozzle or something similar into the lower part of the face and pulling it slightly downwards. His eyes are made by sticking two small discs of white sugarpaste onto his face.

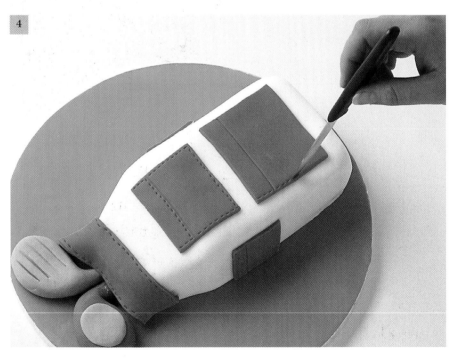

TIP

Personalize the figure by colouring the hair and eyes the same colour as the recipient's. Add any distinguishing features too, such as glasses, a beard or long hair.

Stick two smaller discs of blue onto the white and top with two even smaller discs of black sugarpaste. Stick a tiny ball of flesh-coloured sugarpaste onto the face for his nose and two on either side of the head for his ears. Press the end of a paintbrush into each ear to leave a small hollow. Stick a small oval of flesh-coloured sugarpaste onto the end of each arm for his hands.

10 Make hair by sticking a couple of tiny bits of light brown sugarpaste to the top of the head. To make the cap, roll 10 g (¼ oz) of yellow sugarpaste into a flattish oval shape. Tweak the front into a peak and press lines across the top in a sort of star shape. Top with a tiny ball of yellow sugarpaste and stick on the top of the head. Decorate the front of the jumper and both socks with small, contrasting squares of blue and yellow sugarpaste.

11 To make the strap, thinly roll out 50 g (2 oz) white sugarpaste and cut out a strip about 30 cm x 2.5 cm (12 in x 1 in). 'Stitch' along the edges of the strap in the same way as you did for the pockets, then lay the strap over the top of the bag (fig 7). Use a little water to secure the handle in place.

12 Finally, finish the board with two tiny golf clubs made by rolling about 5 g (⅛ oz) of black sugarpaste into a thin string for the handles. Cut this in half and stick onto the board. Make two tiny golf club heads out of a little brown and grey sugarpaste.

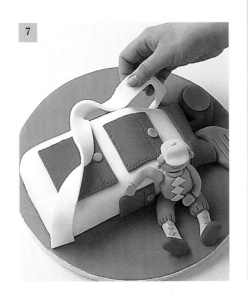

Decorating variation

Another easy sports theme is a sports cap cake. The cake itself was baked in an ovenproof pudding bowl which automatically gave it an authentic rounded shape. It was covered with sugarpaste and a semi-circle of blue sugarpaste was placed on the board to look like its peak. It could be decorated with models from virtually any sport or you could paint a badge or emblem to stick on the front using food colour.

Teddy bear

It is possible to buy a ready-coloured sugarpaste from cake decorating shops that is aptly called 'Teddy Bear Brown'. If you can't get hold of this, use brown sugarpaste mixed with a little yellow and red for a similar colour.

■ INGREDIENTS

- 15 cm (6 in) round sponge cake
- ½ quantity buttercream, (see page 98)
- Icing sugar for rolling out
- 900 g (2 lb) golden brown sugarpaste
- 2 candy sticks or strands of dried spaghetti
- 10 g (¼ oz) white sugarpaste
- 40 g (1¾ oz) black sugarpaste
- Black food colour

■ UTENSILS

- Carving knife
- 20 cm (8 in) round cake board
- Rolling pin
- Small sharp knife
- Water and paintbrush
- Wooden spoon
- 1 m (39 in) ribbon

1 Cut the cake to shape by lying it flat on its base and slicing off about a third of the cake. This section is then placed on top of the remaining cake so that it looks a bit like an 'L' shape from the side.

2 Stick the two sections together with a little buttercream and, if you wish, slice the base cake through the middle and spread a layer of buttercream there as well. Then place the cake towards the rear of the cake board and spread a thin covering of buttercream over the entire cake.

3 Dust the worksurface with icing sugar and knead 300 g (10½ oz) of the golden brown sugarpaste until pliable. Roll the icing out, then lift and place it over the cake. Starting with the tummy area, to stop air bubbles getting trapped there, smooth the icing into position over the cake. You may find that the sugarpaste falls into folds at the back. By gently lifting and pulling the icing you should be able to smooth these out. Trim and neaten the base.

4 To provide support for the head, insert two candy sticks into the top of the body leaving about half the stick protruding (fig 1). If you can't get hold of candy sticks (or sweet cigarettes, as they used to be called), use some shortened strands of raw, dried spaghetti instead. Lightly moisten the area around the candy sticks with water to help keep the head in position, but don't use too much or the head will slide about.

5 Make the head by rolling 300 g (10½ oz) of sugarpaste into a ball. Flatten the ball to make a thick disc and slot the head into position onto the candy sticks.

6 Roll another 90 g (3 oz) of golden brown sugarpaste into an oval for the muzzle. Stick this to the lower part of the face.

7 To make the ears, roll 30 g (1 oz) of golden brown sugarpaste into a ball. Flatten the ball into an oval and cut in half. To add detail, press a rounded hollow into each ear using a wooden spoon handle (fig 2) and stick one either side of the head with a little water.

8 To make the eyes, thinly roll out the white sugarpaste. Cut out two discs and keep the leftover white icing. Stick the circles just above the muzzle. Roll out 10 g (¼ oz) of black sugarpaste and cut out two smaller black discs. Stick these onto the white. Flatten two tiny balls of white sugarpaste. Stick these onto the black as highlights. Finish the face by rolling 10 g (¼ oz) of black sugarpaste into an oval for his nose. Stick this onto the muzzle. Paint a mouth using black food colour.

9 To make the legs, roll two 100 g (3½ oz) lumps of golden brown sugarpaste into chunky carrot shapes. Bend the end of each leg up slightly into an 'L' shape to make a foot and stick the legs into place. Cut two round discs out of the remaining black sugarpaste and stretch them into ovals. Stick one on the pad of each foot.

10 For the paws, roll two 50 g (2 oz) lumps of golden brown sugarpaste into two flattish carrot shapes. Rest the hand sections on the teddy's tummy (fig 3). Using the back of a knife, press a few lines into each paw.

11 For the final finishing touch, tie a ribbon around his neck.

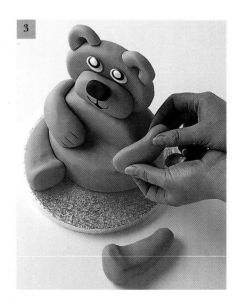

Sunbather

The perfect cake for any beach babe or sun-worshipper – or if your mum's greatest wish is a holiday away from it all, then sending a model of her away on a cake could be the next best thing!

■ INGREDIENTS

- 20 cm (8 in) round sponge cake
- 1 quantity buttercream (see page 98)
- Icing sugar for rolling out
- 500 g (1 lb 2 oz) white sugarpaste
- Blue food colour
- 150 g (5¼ oz) pink sugarpaste
- 30 g (1 oz) dark blue sugarpaste
- 40 g (1¼ oz) flesh-coloured sugarpaste
- 10 g (¼ oz) yellow sugarpaste
- 30 g (1 oz) brown sugarpaste
- 30 g (1 oz) green sugarpaste
- 15 ml (1 tbsp) white royal icing (optional)
- 50 g (2 oz) light golden brown sugar

■ UTENSILS

- 25 cm (10 in) round cake board
- Carving knife
- Small sharp knife
- Rolling pin
- Water and paintbrush
- Piping bag
- No. 3 nozzle

1 Level the top of the cake if necessary. Turn the cake upside down; slice and fill the centre with buttercream. Place on the centre of the cake board and spread a thin layer of buttercream on the top and sides.

2 Dust the worksurface with icing sugar and knead 500 g (1 lb 2 oz) of white sugarpaste until pliable. Partially knead in a little blue food colour for a marbled effect. Roll out, then cover the cake. Smooth the top and sides and trim any excess from the base.

3 For the air-bed, roll out the pink sugarpaste and cut out a rectangle 7 cm x 15 cm (2¾ in x 6 in). Using the back of a knife, press one line horizontally to mark the headrest, then press another five lines vertically down the length of the bed (*fig 1*). Lightly moisten the top of the cake with a little water and place the bed in position.

4 For the figure, take 30 g (1 oz) of dark blue sugarpaste and mould this into a conical shape. Pinch the middle to make a waist (*fig 1*) and stick on top of the air-bed.

5 For the head, roll a ball from 10 g (¼ oz) flesh-coloured sugarpaste. Take another 10 g (¼ oz) of flesh-coloured icing and roll this into a sausage for her arms. Divide this into two and flatten one end of each sausage slightly for the hands. Using 20 g (½ oz) of flesh-coloured icing for the legs, roll into a sausage, divide into two and flatten and shape the ends into feet. Stick the arms, legs and head into position.

6 Roll a small ball of brown sugarpaste out flat and cut out a thin strip for the hair. Press lines along the length of the strip with the back of a knife. For the sun hat, thinly roll out 10 g (¼ oz) of yellow sugarpaste and cut out a 5 cm (2 in) circle. Stick this over the face. Re-knead the leftover yellow and cut out a slightly thicker circle about 3 cm (1 in) in diameter. Stick this on top of the brim. Decorate with a few balls of pink icing.

7 For the palm trees, thinly roll out the brown sugarpaste and cut out about 14 small, curved tree trunks (*fig 2*). Press a few horizontal lines into each with the back of a knife and stick these to the sides of the cake. For the leaves, roll out the green sugarpaste and cut out about 28 basic leaf shapes. Make a few tiny cuts in each leaf. Bend each leaf slightly so that the cuts separate and stick a couple to each trunk.

8 For the waves, place 15 ml (1 tbsp) of royal icing into a piping bag fitted with a number 3 nozzle. Pipe a few lines around the air-bed. Using a damp paintbrush, pull the icing back from the air-bed (*fig 3*). Buttercream can be used as a softer, but

yellower alternative. Stroke into place with a dry brush.

9 Finally, moisten the exposed cake board and spoon brown sugar around the base.

> **TIP**
>
> *If you don't want to make up a full quantity of royal icing just for the waves, buy a tube of ready-made icing from the supermarket which comes with its own set of nozzles.*

Party animal

Here's a party animal who's almost completely partied out! If you're sure that they won't take offence, change the hair colour to match that of the recipient and substitute their favourite tipple for the beer can.

■ INGREDIENTS

- 1 pudding bowl cake (see page 94)
- 1 quantity buttercream (see page 98)
- Icing sugar for rolling out
- 320 g (11 oz) white sugarpaste
- 300 g (10½ oz) pale blue sugarpaste
- 90 g (3 oz) black sugarpaste
- 300 g (10½ oz) flesh-coloured sugarpaste
- 5 g (⅛ oz) dark blue sugarpaste
- 10 g (¼ oz) yellow sugarpaste
- 40 g (1¾ oz) green sugarpaste
- 10 g (¼ oz) grey sugarpaste

■ UTENSILS

- Carving knife and small sharp knife
- 30 cm (12 in) round cake board
- Rolling pin and wooden spoon
- Water and paintbrush
- Piping nozzle

1 Check that the cake will sit flat on the cake board when it is turned upside down. If the cake rose slightly unevenly in the oven, you may need to slice a little away from the top. Place the cake towards the back of the board, rounded side uppermost, and slice and fill the centre with buttercream. Reassemble the cake and spread a layer of buttercream over the outside.

2 Dust the worksurface with icing sugar. Knead 100 g (3½ oz) of white sugarpaste until it becomes pliable. Roll it out, then place it so that it covers just over half of the cake. Smooth and trim the base.

3 Roll out 100 g (3½ oz) of the pale blue sugarpaste. Lift and position this so that it overlaps the white. Smooth it into position, and again trim and neaten the base.

4 For the legs, roll 200 g (7 oz) of blue sugarpaste into a thick sausage about 20 cm (8 in) long. Cut it in half. Moisten the board and place the legs into position.

5 Using 200 g (7 oz) of white sugarpaste, make the arms in the same way as the legs. Stick them in position, pointing them forwards towards the front of the board.

6 For the feet, divide a 60 g (2 oz) ball of black sugarpaste in two and roll each half into a chunky oval shape. Stick one to the end of each foot with water, positioning them in a pigeon-toed fashion *(fig 1)*. To add detail, press the back of a knife into the sole of each foot a few times.

7 For the hands, take 50 g (1¾ oz) of flesh-coloured sugarpaste and roll into a thick oval shape. Cut the oval in half and using the back of a knife, press four lines into the rounded ends to make fingers. Stick the hands in place. His right one should be flat on the board and his left one on its side and curved, to hold the beer can!

8 To make his face, roll 200 g (7 oz) of flesh-coloured sugarpaste into a ball. Flatten the ball into a rounded disc about 11 cm (41 in) in diameter. Moisten the side of the cake and the board in front of the cake with water and lay the disc into position.

9 Make his smile by drawing a line with the back of a knife. For his eyes, roll out 10 g (¼ oz) of white sugarpaste and cut out two small circles 2.5 cm (1 in) in diameter. Stick these on the face. Roll out 5 g (⅛ oz) of black sugarpaste and cut out two smaller discs. Stick the black circles onto the white *(fig 2)*. Complete by sticking on a flattened ball of white sugarpaste as a highlight.

10 For the eyelids, roll out 10 g (¼ oz) of flesh-coloured sugarpaste and cut a circle about 4.5 cm (1¾ in) in diameter. Cut the circle in two and stick one half over each eye to create a droopy-eyed expression.

11 Take a 20 g (¾ oz) ball of flesh-coloured sugarpaste and slightly flatten it. Stick it in the middle of the face to make his nose.

12 For his hair, roll 20 g (¾ oz) of black sugarpaste into a long thin strip. Press the back of a knife along the length of the strip, then moisten the top of the head with water and lay the strip in place.

13 For the ears, roll 20 g (¾ oz) of flesh-coloured sugarpaste into a ball. Flatten it and push the end of a wooden spoon into the centre to leave a hollow. Cut the circle in half and stick both ears onto the head.

14 For the hat, roll the dark blue sugarpaste into a triangle. Stick this at an angle on top of his head. Roll the yellow sugarpaste into thin strings and stick to the hat.

15 To make the can, roll the green sugarpaste into a sausage. Flatten both ends. Cut out two flat discs from grey sugarpaste the same size as the beer can. Sandwich the green between the two grey discs and stick a small triangle of black sugarpaste onto the top of the can. Place in position.

Deep sea fishing

Here's one to hook a hungry fisherman! If you prefer a softer sea, substitute buttercream for the royal icing, but use unsalted butter as this produces a whiter buttercream which takes the colour better. You could also personalize the fisherman if you wish.

1   Turn the cake upside down and carefully carve the front of the cake into a rounded shape. Slice the cake and fill the centre with buttercream. Place the cake in position on the cake board and spread a thin layer of buttercream around the top and sides.

2   Dust the worksurface with a little icing sugar and roll out 350 g (12 oz) of grey sugarpaste. Lift this over the cake and ease it into place, using cake smoothers if you possess them to achieve an extra smooth finish on the sugarpaste. Alternatively, use the palms of your hands.

   Trim and neaten the base, keeping the excess sugarpaste for making the tail. Using the back of your knife, press a curved line into the front of the whale to make a sneaky, smiley mouth (*fig 1*).

3   To make the eyes, roll out about 5 g (⅛ oz) of white sugarpaste. Using a circle cutter

or a lid of some sort, cut out two flat discs about 2.5 cm (1 in) wide. (If you cannot find a cutter of the right size, simply squash two small balls of white sugarpaste instead.) Stick one either side of the face with a little water.

   Roll out a small lump of black sugarpaste and cut out two smaller discs (a piping nozzle makes an ideal cutter for these). Stick the black discs onto the white. Flatten two tiny balls of white sugarpaste and stick these onto the black discs to look like highlights.

   Finally, to finish the eyes, roll out 10 g (¼ oz) of grey sugarpaste and cut out a disc approximately 4.5 cm (1¾ in) wide. Cut this in half and stick one half over each eye (*fig 2*).

4   Make the rocks by partially kneading together 150 g (5 oz) of white sugarpaste and 40 g (1¾ oz) of black sugarpaste (refer to the Wild Animals cake on page 16 for

more details if you're unsure how to do this). Pull off lumps of various sizes and mould these into rock shapes. Make sure that the largest, which the fisherman will sit on, has a flattish top so that he doesn't fall off! Place the rocks to one side.

5   To avoid any accidents, make the fisherman on his rock away from the board. Roll 5 g (⅛ oz) of black sugarpaste into a sausage. Cut it in half for his legs and bend the end of each leg up to make a foot (*fig 3*). Stick both the feet onto the largest rock. Roll 5 g (⅛ oz) of green sugarpaste into an oval for his body. Stick this above the legs.

INGREDIENTS

- 1 pudding basin cake (see page 94)
- 1 quantity buttercream (see page 98)
- Icing sugar for rolling out
- 400 g (14 oz) grey sugarpaste
- 180 g (6 oz) white sugarpaste
- 50 g (2 oz) black sugarpaste
- 10 g (¼ oz) green sugarpaste
- 10 g (¼ oz) flesh-coloured sugarpaste
- Black and blue food colours
- 10 g (¼ oz) yellow sugarpaste
- ½ quantity royal icing (see page 99)

UTENSILS

- Carving knife
- 25 cm (10 in) square cake board
- Rolling pin
- Cake smoothers (optional)
- Small sharp knife
- Circle cutters or similar for cutting out eyes
- Water, and fine and medium paintbrushes
- Drinking straw
- White cotton thread
- Cocktail stick
- Small bowl and palette knife
- Piping bag, if making waves

TIP

Remember to remove the thread and cocktail stick when cutting the cake, especially if there are children around.